W9-AOI-517

BUSINESS MATH HANDBOOK AND STUDY GUIDE

to accompany

PRACTICAL BUSINESS MATH PROCEDURES

Jeffrey Slater
North Shore Community College
Danvers, Massachusetts

Eighth Edition

McGraw-Hill
Irwin

Boston   Burr Ridge, IL   Dubuque, IA   Madison, WI   New York   San Francisco   St. Louis
Bangkok   Bogotá   Caracas   Kuala Lumpur   Lisbon   London   Madrid   Mexico City
Milan   Montreal   New Delhi   Santiago   Seoul   Singapore   Sydney   Taipei   Toronto

The McGraw·Hill Companies

Business Math Handbook and Study Guide to accompany
PRACTICAL BUSINESS MATH PROCEDURES

Copyright © 2006, 2003, 2000, 1997, 1994, 1991 by The McGraw-Hill Companies, Inc. All rights reserved.
Printed in the United States of America.
The contents of, or parts thereof, may be reproduced for use with
PRACTICAL BUSINESS MATH PROCEDURES, 8/e
Slater
provided such reproductions bear copyright notice and may not be reproduced in
any form for any other purpose without permission of the publisher.

2 3 4 5 6 7 8 9 0 QPD/QPD 0 9 8 7 6 5

ISBN 0-07-296722-6

http://www.mhhe.com

PERIOD	COMPOUND INTEREST	PRESENT VALUE	AMOUNT OF ANNUITY	PRESENT VALUE OF ANNUITY	SINKING FUND
1	1.0050	0.9950	1.0000	0.9950	1.0000
2	1.0100	0.9901	2.0050	1.9851	0.4988
3	1.0151	0.9851	3.0150	2.9702	0.3317
4	1.0202	0.9802	4.0301	3.9505	0.2481
5	1.0253	0.9754	5.0503	4.9259	0.1980
6	1.0304	0.9705	6.0755	5.8964	0.1646
7	1.0355	0.9657	7.1059	6.8621	0.1407
8	1.0407	0.9609	8.1414	7.8230	0.1228
9	1.0459	0.9561	9.1821	8.7791	0.1089
10	1.0511	0.9513	10.2280	9.7304	0.0978
11	1.0564	0.9466	11.2792	10.6770	0.0887
12	1.0617	0.9419	12.3356	11.6189	0.0811
13	1.0670	0.9372	13.3973	12.5562	0.0746
14	1.0723	0.9326	14.4643	13.4887	0.0691
15	1.0777	0.9279	15.5365	14.4166	0.0644
16	1.0831	0.9233	16.6142	15.3399	0.0602
17	1.0885	0.9187	17.6973	16.2586	0.0565
18	1.0939	0.9141	18.7858	17.1728	0.0532
19	1.0994	0.9096	19.8797	18.0824	0.0503
20	1.1049	0.9051	20.9791	18.9874	0.0477
21	1.1104	0.9006	22.0840	19.8880	0.0453
22	1.1160	0.8961	23.1945	20.7841	0.0431
23	1.1216	0.8916	24.3104	21.6757	0.0411
24	1.1272	0.8872	25.4320	22.5629	0.0393
25	1.1328	0.8828	26.5591	23.4457	0.0377
26	1.1385	0.8784	27.6919	24.3240	0.0361
27	1.1442	0.8740	28.8304	25.1980	0.0347
28	1.1499	0.8697	29.9746	26.0677	0.0334
29	1.1556	0.8653	31.1245	26.9331	0.0321
30	1.1614	0.8610	32.2801	27.7941	0.0310
31	1.1672	0.8567	33.4414	28.6508	0.0299
32	1.1730	0.8525	34.6087	29.5033	0.0289
33	1.1789	0.8482	35.7817	30.3515	0.0279
34	1.1848	0.8440	36.9606	31.1956	0.0271
35	1.1907	0.8398	38.1454	32.0354	0.0262
36	1.1967	0.8356	39.3361	32.8710	0.0254
37	1.2027	0.8315	40.5328	33.7025	0.0247
38	1.2087	0.8274	41.7355	34.5299	0.0240
39	1.2147	0.8232	42.9441	35.3531	0.0233
40	1.2208	0.8191	44.1589	36.1723	0.0226
41	1.2269	0.8151	45.3797	36.9873	0.0220
42	1.2330	0.8110	46.6066	37.7983	0.0215
43	1.2392	0.8070	47.8396	38.6053	0.0209
44	1.2454	0.8030	49.0788	39.4083	0.0204
45	1.2516	0.7990	50.3242	40.2072	0.0199
46	1.2579	0.7950	51.5759	41.0022	0.0194
47	1.2642	0.7910	52.8337	41.7932	0.0189
48	1.2705	0.7871	54.0979	42.5804	0.0185
49	1.2768	0.7832	55.3684	43.3635	0.0181
50	1.2832	0.7793	56.6452	44.1428	0.0177

1

1%

PERIOD	COMPOUND INTEREST	PRESENT VALUE	AMOUNT OF ANNUITY	PRESENT VALUE OF ANNUITY	SINKING FUND
1	1.0100	0.9901	1.0000	0.9901	1.0000
2	1.0201	0.9803	2.0100	1.9704	0.4975
3	1.0303	0.9706	3.0301	2.9410	0.3300
4	1.0406	0.9610	4.0604	3.9020	0.2463
5	1.0510	0.9515	5.1010	4.8534	0.1960
6	1.0615	0.9420	6.1520	5.7955	0.1625
7	1.0721	0.9327	7.2135	6.7282	0.1386
8	1.0829	0.9235	8.2857	7.6517	0.1207
9	1.0937	0.9143	9.3685	8.5660	0.1067
10	1.1046	0.9053	10.4622	9.4713	0.0956
11	1.1157	0.8963	11.5668	10.3676	0.0865
12	1.1268	0.8874	12.6825	11.2551	0.0788
13	1.1381	0.8787	13.8093	12.1337	0.0724
14	1.1495	0.8700	14.9474	13.0037	0.0669
15	1.1610	0.8613	16.0969	13.8650	0.0621
16	1.1726	0.8528	17.2579	14.7179	0.0579
17	1.1843	0.8444	18.4304	15.5622	0.0543
18	1.1961	0.8360	19.6147	16.3983	0.0510
19	1.2081	0.8277	20.8109	17.2260	0.0481
20	1.2202	0.8195	22.0190	18.0455	0.0454
21	1.2324	0.8114	23.2392	18.8570	0.0430
22	1.2447	0.8034	24.4716	19.6604	0.0409
23	1.2572	0.7954	25.7163	20.4558	0.0389
24	1.2697	0.7876	26.9735	21.2434	0.0371
25	1.2824	0.7798	28.2432	22.0231	0.0354
26	1.2953	0.7720	29.5256	22.7952	0.0339
27	1.3082	0.7644	30.8209	23.5596	0.0324
28	1.3213	0.7568	32.1291	24.3164	0.0311
29	1.3345	0.7493	33.4504	25.0658	0.0299
30	1.3478	0.7419	34.7849	25.8077	0.0287
31	1.3613	0.7346	36.1327	26.5423	0.0277
32	1.3749	0.7273	37.4941	27.2696	0.0267
33	1.3887	0.7201	38.8690	27.9897	0.0257
34	1.4026	0.7130	40.2577	28.7027	0.0248
35	1.4166	0.7059	41.6603	29.4086	0.0240
36	1.4308	0.6989	43.0769	30.1075	0.0232
37	1.4451	0.6920	44.5076	30.7995	0.0225
38	1.4595	0.6852	45.9527	31.4847	0.0218
39	1.4741	0.6784	47.4122	32.1630	0.0211
40	1.4889	0.6717	48.8864	32.8347	0.0205
41	1.5038	0.6650	50.3752	33.4997	0.0199
42	1.5188	0.6584	51.8790	34.1581	0.0193
43	1.5340	0.6519	53.3978	34.8100	0.0187
44	1.5493	0.6454	54.9317	35.4554	0.0182
45	1.5648	0.6391	56.4811	36.0945	0.0177
46	1.5805	0.6327	58.0459	36.7272	0.0172
47	1.5963	0.6265	59.6263	37.3537	0.0168
48	1.6122	0.6203	61.2226	37.9739	0.0163
49	1.6283	0.6141	62.8348	38.5881	0.0159
50	1.6446	0.6080	64.4632	39.1961	0.0155

PERIOD	COMPOUND INTEREST	PRESENT VALUE	AMOUNT OF ANNUITY	PRESENT VALUE OF ANNUITY	SINKING FUND
1	1.0150	0.9852	1.0000	0.9852	1.0000
2	1.0302	0.9707	2.0150	1.9559	0.4963
3	1.0457	0.9563	3.0452	2.9122	0.3284
4	1.0614	0.9422	4.0909	3.8544	0.2444
5	1.0773	0.9283	5.1522	4.7826	0.1941
6	1.0934	0.9145	6.2295	5.6972	0.1605
7	1.1098	0.9010	7.3230	6.5982	0.1366
8	1.1265	0.8877	8.4328	7.4859	0.1186
9	1.1434	0.8746	9.5593	8.3605	0.1046
10	1.1605	0.8617	10.7027	9.2222	0.0934
11	1.1780	0.8489	11.8632	10.0711	0.0843
12	1.1960	0.8364	13.0412	10.9075	0.0767
13	1.2135	0.8240	14.2368	11.7315	0.0702
14	1.2318	0.8119	15.4503	12.5433	0.0647
15	1.2502	0.7999	16.6821	13.3432	0.0599
16	1.2690	0.7880	17.9323	14.1312	0.0558
17	1.2880	0.7764	19.2013	14.9076	0.0521
18	1.3073	0.7649	20.4893	15.6725	0.0488
19	1.3270	0.7536	21.7966	16.4261	0.0459
20	1.3469	0.7425	23.1236	17.1686	0.0432
21	1.3671	0.7315	24.4704	17.9001	0.0409
22	1.3876	0.7207	25.8375	18.6208	0.0387
23	1.4084	0.7100	27.2250	19.3308	0.0367
24	1.4295	0.6995	28.6334	20.0304	0.0349
25	1.4510	0.6892	30.0629	20.7196	0.0333
26	1.4727	0.6790	31.5138	21.3986	0.0317
27	1.4948	0.6690	32.9866	22.0676	0.0303
28	1.5172	0.6591	34.4813	22.7267	0.0290
29	1.5400	0.6494	35.9986	23.3760	0.0278
30	1.5631	0.6398	37.5385	24.0158	0.0266
31	1.5865	0.6303	39.1016	24.6461	0.0256
32	1.6103	0.6210	40.6881	25.2671	0.0246
33	1.6345	0.6118	42.2984	25.8789	0.0236
34	1.6590	0.6028	43.9329	26.4817	0.0228
35	1.6839	0.5939	45.5919	27.0755	0.0219
36	1.7091	0.5851	47.2758	27.6606	0.0212
37	1.7348	0.5764	48.9849	28.2371	0.0204
38	1.7608	0.5679	50.7197	28.8050	0.0197
39	1.7872	0.5595	52.4805	29.3645	0.0191
40	1.8140	0.5513	54.2677	29.9158	0.0184
41	1.8412	0.5431	56.0817	30.4589	0.0178
42	1.8688	0.5351	57.9229	30.9940	0.0173
43	1.8969	0.5272	59.7917	31.5212	0.0167
44	1.9253	0.5194	61.6886	32.0405	0.0162
45	1.9542	0.5117	63.6139	32.5523	0.0157
46	1.9835	0.5042	65.5681	33.0564	0.0153
47	2.0133	0.4967	67.5516	33.5531	0.0148
48	2.0435	0.4894	69.5649	34.0425	0.0144
49	2.0741	0.4821	71.6084	34.5246	0.0140
50	2.1052	0.4750	73.6825	34.9996	0.0136

2%

PERIOD	COMPOUND INTEREST	PRESENT VALUE	AMOUNT OF ANNUITY	PRESENT VALUE OF ANNUITY	SINKING FUND
1	1.0200	0.9804	1.0000	0.9804	1.0000
2	1.0404	0.9612	2.0200	1.9416	0.4951
3	1.0612	0.9423	3.0604	2.8839	0.3268
4	1.0824	0.9238	4.1216	3.8077	0.2426
5	1.1041	0.9057	5.2040	4.7134	0.1922
6	1.1262	0.8880	6.3081	5.6014	0.1585
7	1.1487	0.8706	7.4343	6.4720	0.1345
8	1.1717	0.8535	8.5829	7.3255	0.1165
9	1.1951	0.8368	9.7546	8.1622	0.1025
10	1.2190	0.8203	10.9497	8.9826	0.0913
11	1.2434	0.8043	12.1687	9.7868	0.0822
12	1.2682	0.7885	13.4120	10.5753	0.0746
13	1.2936	0.7730	14.6803	11.3483	0.0681
14	1.3195	0.7579	15.9739	12.1062	0.0626
15	1.3459	0.7430	17.2934	12.8492	0.0578
16	1.3728	0.7284	18.6392	13.5777	0.0537
17	1.4002	0.7142	20.0120	14.2918	0.0500
18	1.4282	0.7002	21.4122	14.9920	0.0467
19	1.4568	0.6864	22.8405	15.6784	0.0438
20	1.4859	0.6730	24.2973	16.3514	0.0412
21	1.5157	0.6598	25.7832	17.0112	0.0388
22	1.5460	0.6468	27.2989	17.6580	0.0366
23	1.5769	0.6342	28.8449	18.2922	0.0347
24	1.6084	0.6217	30.4218	18.9139	0.0329
25	1.6406	0.6095	32.0302	19.5234	0.0312
26	1.6734	0.5976	33.6708	20.1210	0.0297
27	1.7069	0.5859	35.3442	20.7069	0.0283
28	1.7410	0.5744	37.0511	21.2812	0.0270
29	1.7758	0.5631	38.7921	21.8443	0.0258
30	1.8114	0.5521	40.5679	22.3964	0.0247
31	1.8476	0.5412	42.3793	22.9377	0.0236
32	1.8845	0.5306	44.2269	23.4683	0.0226
33	1.9222	0.5202	46.1114	23.9885	0.0217
34	1.9607	0.5100	48.0336	24.4985	0.0208
35	1.9999	0.5000	49.9943	24.9986	0.0200
36	2.0399	0.4902	51.9942	25.4888	0.0192
37	2.0807	0.4806	54.0340	25.9694	0.0185
38	2.1223	0.4712	56.1147	26.4406	0.0178
39	2.1647	0.4619	58.2370	26.9025	0.0172
40	2.2080	0.4529	60.4017	27.3554	0.0166
41	2.2522	0.4440	62.6098	27.7994	0.0160
42	2.2972	0.4353	64.8620	28.2347	0.0154
43	2.3432	0.4268	67.1592	28.6615	0.0149
44	2.3900	0.4184	69.5024	29.0799	0.0144
45	2.4378	0.4102	71.8924	29.4901	0.0139
46	2.4866	0.4022	74.3302	29.8923	0.0135
47	2.5363	0.3943	76.8168	30.2865	0.0130
48	2.5871	0.3865	79.3532	30.6731	0.0126
49	2.6388	0.3790	81.9402	31.0520	0.0122
50	2.6916	0.3715	84.5790	31.4236	0.0118

4

PERIOD	COMPOUND INTEREST	PRESENT VALUE	AMOUNT OF ANNUITY	PRESENT VALUE OF ANNUITY	SINKING FUND
1	1.0250	0.9756	1.0000	0.9756	1.0000
2	1.0506	0.9518	2.0250	1.9274	0.4938
3	1.0769	0.9286	3.0756	2.8560	0.3251
4	1.1038	0.9060	4.1525	3.7620	0.2408
5	1.1314	0.8839	5.2563	4.6458	0.1902
6	1.1597	0.8623	6.3877	5.5081	0.1566
7	1.1887	0.8413	7.5474	6.3494	0.1325
8	1.2184	0.8207	8.7361	7.1701	0.1145
9	1.2489	0.8007	9.9545	7.9709	0.1005
10	1.2801	0.7812	11.2034	8.7521	0.0893
11	1.3121	0.7621	12.4835	9.5142	0.0801
12	1.3449	0.7436	13.7955	10.2578	0.0725
13	1.3785	0.7254	15.1404	10.9832	0.0660
14	1.4130	0.7077	16.5189	11.6909	0.0605
15	1.4483	0.6905	17.9319	12.3814	0.0558
16	1.4845	0.6736	19.3802	13.0550	0.0516
17	1.5216	0.6572	20.8647	13.7122	0.0479
18	1.5597	0.6412	22.3863	14.3534	0.0447
19	1.5986	0.6255	23.9460	14.9789	0.0418
20	1.6386	0.6103	25.5446	15.5892	0.0391
21	1.6796	0.5954	27.1832	16.1845	0.0368
22	1.7216	0.5809	28.8628	16.7654	0.0346
23	1.7646	0.5667	30.5844	17.3321	0.0327
24	1.8087	0.5529	32.3490	17.8850	0.0309
25	1.8539	0.5394	34.1577	18.4244	0.0293
26	1.9003	0.5262	36.0117	18.9506	0.0278
27	1.9478	0.5134	37.9120	19.4640	0.0264
28	1.9965	0.5009	39.8598	19.9649	0.0251
29	2.0464	0.4887	41.8563	20.4535	0.0239
30	2.0976	0.4767	43.9027	20.9303	0.0228
31	2.1500	0.4651	46.0002	21.3954	0.0217
32	2.2038	0.4538	48.1502	21.8492	0.0208
33	2.2588	0.4427	50.3540	22.2919	0.0199
34	2.3153	0.4319	52.6128	22.7238	0.0190
35	2.3732	0.4214	54.9282	23.1451	0.0182
36	2.4325	0.4111	57.3014	23.5562	0.0175
37	2.4933	0.4011	59.7339	23.9573	0.0167
38	2.5557	0.3913	62.2272	24.3486	0.0161
39	2.6196	0.3817	64.7829	24.7303	0.0154
40	2.6851	0.3724	67.4025	25.1028	0.0148
41	2.7522	0.3633	70.0875	25.4661	0.0143
42	2.8210	0.3545	72.8397	25.8206	0.0137
43	2.8915	0.3458	75.6607	26.1664	0.0132
44	2.9638	0.3374	78.5522	26.5038	0.0127
45	3.0379	0.3292	81.5160	26.8330	0.0123
46	3.1138	0.3211	84.5539	27.1542	0.0118
47	3.1917	0.3133	87.6678	27.4675	0.0114
48	3.2715	0.3057	90.8595	27.7731	0.0110
49	3.3533	0.2982	94.1310	28.0714	0.0106
50	3.4371	0.2909	97.4842	28.3623	0.0103

3%

PERIOD	COMPOUND INTEREST	PRESENT VALUE	AMOUNT OF ANNUITY	PRESENT VALUE OF ANNUITY	SINKING FUND
1	1.0300	0.9709	1.0000	0.9709	1.0000
2	1.0609	0.9426	2.0300	1.9135	0.4926
3	1.0927	0.9151	3.0909	2.8286	0.3235
4	1.1255	0.8885	4.1836	3.7171	0.2390
5	1.1593	0.8626	5.3091	4.5797	0.1884
6	1.1941	0.8375	6.4684	5.4172	0.1546
7	1.2299	0.8131	7.6625	6.2303	0.1305
8	1.2668	0.7894	8.8923	7.0197	0.1125
9	1.3048	0.7664	10.1591	7.7861	0.0984
10	1.3439	0.7441	11.4639	8.5302	0.0872
11	1.3842	0.7224	12.8078	9.2526	0.0781
12	1.4258	0.7014	14.1920	9.9540	0.0705
13	1.4685	0.6810	15.6178	10.6350	0.0640
14	1.5126	0.6611	17.0863	11.2961	0.0585
15	1.5580	0.6419	18.5989	11.9379	0.0538
16	1.6047	0.6232	20.1569	12.5611	0.0496
17	1.6528	0.6050	21.7616	13.1661	0.0460
18	1.7024	0.5874	23.4144	13.7535	0.0427
19	1.7535	0.5703	25.1169	14.3238	0.0398
20	1.8061	0.5537	26.8704	14.8775	0.0372
21	1.8603	0.5375	28.6765	15.4150	0.0349
22	1.9161	0.5219	30.5368	15.9369	0.0327
23	1.9736	0.5067	32.4529	16.4436	0.0308
24	2.0328	0.4919	34.4265	16.9355	0.0290
25	2.0938	0.4776	36.4593	17.4131	0.0274
26	2.1566	0.4637	38.5530	17.8768	0.0259
27	2.2213	0.4502	40.7096	18.3270	0.0246
28	2.2879	0.4371	42.9309	18.7641	0.0233
29	2.3566	0.4243	45.2188	19.1885	0.0221
30	2.4273	0.4120	47.5754	19.6004	0.0210
31	2.5001	0.4000	50.0027	20.0004	0.0200
32	2.5751	0.3883	52.5027	20.3888	0.0190
33	2.6523	0.3770	55.0778	20.7658	0.0182
34	2.7319	0.3660	57.7302	21.1318	0.0173
35	2.8139	0.3554	60.4621	21.4872	0.0165
36	2.8983	0.3450	63.2759	21.8323	0.0158
37	2.9852	0.3350	66.1742	22.1672	0.0151
38	3.0748	0.3252	69.1594	22.4925	0.0145
39	3.1670	0.3158	72.2342	22.8082	0.0138
40	3.2620	0.3066	75.4012	23.1148	0.0133
41	3.3599	0.2976	78.6633	23.4124	0.0127
42	3.4607	0.2890	82.0232	23.7014	0.0122
43	3.5645	0.2805	85.4839	23.9819	0.0117
44	3.6715	0.2724	89.0484	24.2543	0.0112
45	3.7816	0.2644	92.7198	24.5187	0.0108
46	3.8950	0.2567	96.5014	24.7754	0.0104
47	4.0119	0.2493	100.3965	25.0247	0.0100
48	4.1323	0.2420	104.4084	25.2667	0.0096
49	4.2562	0.2350	108.5406	25.5017	0.0092
50	4.3839	0.2281	112.7968	25.7298	0.0089

PERIOD	COMPOUND INTEREST	PRESENT VALUE	AMOUNT OF ANNUITY	PRESENT VALUE OF ANNUITY	SINKING FUND
1	1.0350	0.9662	1.0000	0.9662	1.0000
2	1.0712	0.9335	2.0350	1.8997	0.4914
3	1.1087	0.9019	3.1062	2.8016	0.3219
4	1.1475	0.8714	4.2149	3.6731	0.2373
5	1.1877	0.8420	5.3625	4.5150	0.1865
6	1.2293	0.8135	6.5501	5.3285	0.1527
7	1.2723	0.7860	7.7794	6.1145	0.1285
8	1.3168	0.7594	9.0517	6.8739	0.1105
9	1.3629	0.7337	10.3685	7.6077	0.0964
10	1.4106	0.7089	11.7314	8.3166	0.0852
11	1.4600	0.6849	13.1420	9.0015	0.0761
12	1.5111	0.6618	14.6019	9.6633	0.0685
13	1.5640	0.6394	16.1130	10.3027	0.0621
14	1.6187	0.6178	17.6770	10.9205	0.0566
15	1.6753	0.5969	19.2957	11.5174	0.0518
16	1.7340	0.5767	20.9710	12.0941	0.0477
17	1.7947	0.5572	22.7050	12.6513	0.0440
18	1.8575	0.5384	24.4997	13.1897	0.0408
19	1.9225	0.5202	26.3571	13.7098	0.0379
20	1.9898	0.5026	28.2796	14.2124	0.0354
21	2.0594	0.4856	30.2694	14.6980	0.0330
22	2.1315	0.4692	32.3288	15.1671	0.0309
23	2.2061	0.4533	34.4604	15.6204	0.0290
24	2.2833	0.4380	36.6665	16.0584	0.0273
25	2.3632	0.4231	38.9498	16.4815	0.0257
26	2.4460	0.4088	41.3130	16.8903	0.0242
27	2.5316	0.3950	43.7590	17.2854	0.0229
28	2.6202	0.3817	46.2905	17.6670	0.0216
29	2.7119	0.3687	48.9107	18.0358	0.0204
30	2.8068	0.3563	51.6226	18.3920	0.0194
31	2.9050	0.3442	54.4294	18.7363	0.0184
32	3.0067	0.3326	57.3344	19.0689	0.0174
33	3.1119	0.3213	60.3411	19.3902	0.0166
34	3.2209	0.3105	63.4530	19.7007	0.0158
35	3.3336	0.3000	66.6739	20.0007	0.0150
36	3.4503	0.2898	70.0075	20.2905	0.0143
37	3.5710	0.2800	73.4577	20.5705	0.0136
38	3.6960	0.2706	77.0287	20.8411	0.0130
39	3.8254	0.2614	80.7247	21.1025	0.0124
40	3.9593	0.2526	84.5501	21.3551	0.0118
41	4.0978	0.2440	88.5093	21.5991	0.0113
42	4.2413	0.2358	92.6072	21.8349	0.0108
43	4.3897	0.2278	96.8484	22.0627	0.0103
44	4.5433	0.2201	101.2381	22.2828	0.0099
45	4.7023	0.2127	105.7814	22.4954	0.0095
46	4.8669	0.2055	110.4838	22.7009	0.0091
47	5.0373	0.1985	115.3507	22.8994	0.0087
48	5.2136	0.1918	120.3880	23.0912	0.0083
49	5.3961	0.1853	125.6015	23.2766	0.0080
50	5.5849	0.1791	130.9976	23.4556	0.0076

4%

PERIOD	COMPOUND INTEREST	PRESENT VALUE	AMOUNT OF ANNUITY	PRESENT VALUE OF ANNUITY	SINKING FUND
1	1.0400	0.9615	1.0000	0.9615	1.0000
2	1.0816	0.9246	2.0400	1.8861	0.4902
3	1.1249	0.8890	3.1216	2.7751	0.3203
4	1.1699	0.8548	4.2465	3.6299	0.2355
5	1.2167	0.8219	5.4163	4.4518	0.1846
6	1.2653	0.7903	6.6330	5.2421	0.1508
7	1.3159	0.7599	7.8983	6.0021	0.1266
8	1.3686	0.7307	9.2142	6.7327	0.1085
9	1.4233	0.7026	10.5828	7.4353	0.0945
10	1.4802	0.6756	12.0061	8.1109	0.0833
11	1.5395	0.6496	13.4863	8.7605	0.0741
12	1.6010	0.6246	15.0258	9.3851	0.0666
13	1.6651	0.6006	16.6268	9.9856	0.0601
14	1.7317	0.5775	18.2919	10.5631	0.0547
15	1.8009	0.5553	20.0236	11.1184	0.0499
16	1.8730	0.5339	21.8245	11.6523	0.0458
17	1.9479	0.5134	23.6975	12.1657	0.0422
18	2.0258	0.4936	25.6454	12.6593	0.0390
19	2.1068	0.4746	27.6712	13.1339	0.0361
20	2.1911	0.4564	29.7781	13.5903	0.0336
21	2.2788	0.4388	31.9692	14.0292	0.0313
22	2.3699	0.4220	34.2479	14.4511	0.0292
23	2.4647	0.4057	36.6179	14.8568	0.0273
24	2.5633	0.3901	39.0826	15.2470	0.0256
25	2.6658	0.3751	41.6459	15.6221	0.0240
26	2.7725	0.3607	44.3117	15.9828	0.0226
27	2.8834	0.3468	47.0842	16.3296	0.0212
28	2.9987	0.3335	49.9675	16.6631	0.0200
29	3.1187	0.3207	52.9662	16.9837	0.0189
30	3.2434	0.3083	56.0849	17.2920	0.0178
31	3.3731	0.2965	59.3283	17.5885	0.0169
32	3.5081	0.2851	62.7014	17.8735	0.0159
33	3.6484	0.2741	66.2095	18.1476	0.0151
34	3.7943	0.2636	69.8578	18.4112	0.0143
35	3.9461	0.2534	73.6521	18.6646	0.0136
36	4.1039	0.2437	77.5982	18.9083	0.0129
37	4.2681	0.2343	81.7022	19.1426	0.0122
38	4.4388	0.2253	85.9702	19.3679	0.0116
39	4.6164	0.2166	90.4091	19.5845	0.0111
40	4.8010	0.2083	95.0254	19.7928	0.0105
41	4.9931	0.2003	99.8264	19.9930	0.0100
42	5.1928	0.1926	104.8195	20.1856	0.0095
43	5.4005	0.1852	110.0122	20.3708	0.0091
44	5.6165	0.1780	115.4127	20.5488	0.0087
45	5.8412	0.1712	121.0292	20.7200	0.0083
46	6.0748	0.1646	126.8704	20.8847	0.0079
47	6.3178	0.1583	132.9452	21.0429	0.0075
48	6.5705	0.1522	139.2630	21.1951	0.0072
49	6.8333	0.1463	145.8335	21.3415	0.0069
50	7.1067	0.1407	152.6669	21.4822	0.0066

PERIOD	COMPOUND INTEREST	PRESENT VALUE	AMOUNT OF ANNUITY	PRESENT VALUE OF ANNUITY	SINKING FUND
1	1.0450	0.9569	1.0000	0.9569	1.0000
2	1.0920	0.9157	2.0450	1.8727	0.4890
3	1.1412	0.8763	3.1370	2.7490	0.3188
4	1.1925	0.8386	4.2782	3.5875	0.2337
5	1.2462	0.8025	5.4707	4.3900	0.1828
6	1.3023	0.7679	6.7169	5.1579	0.1489
7	1.3609	0.7348	8.0191	5.8927	0.1247
8	1.4221	0.7032	9.3800	6.5959	0.1066
9	1.4861	0.6729	10.8021	7.2688	0.0926
10	1.5530	0.6439	12.2882	7.9127	0.0814
11	1.6229	0.6162	13.8412	8.5289	0.0722
12	1.6959	0.5897	15.4640	9.1186	0.0647
13	1.7722	0.5643	17.1599	9.6828	0.0583
14	1.8519	0.5400	18.9321	10.2228	0.0528
15	1.9353	0.5167	20.7840	10.7395	0.0481
16	2.0224	0.4945	22.7193	11.2340	0.0440
17	2.1134	0.4732	24.7417	11.7072	0.0404
18	2.2085	0.4528	26.8551	12.1600	0.0372
19	2.3079	0.4333	29.0635	12.5933	0.0344
20	2.4117	0.4146	31.3714	13.0079	0.0319
21	2.5202	0.3968	33.7831	13.4047	0.0296
22	2.6337	0.3797	36.3033	13.7844	0.0275
23	2.7522	0.3634	38.9370	14.1478	0.0257
24	2.8760	0.3477	41.6892	14.4955	0.0240
25	3.0054	0.3327	44.5652	14.8282	0.0224
26	3.1407	0.3184	47.5706	15.1466	0.0210
27	3.2820	0.3047	50.7113	15.4513	0.0197
28	3.4297	0.2916	53.9933	15.7429	0.0185
29	3.5840	0.2790	57.4230	16.0219	0.0174
30	3.7453	0.2670	61.0070	16.2889	0.0164
31	3.9139	0.2555	64.7523	16.5444	0.0154
32	4.0900	0.2445	68.6662	16.7889	0.0146
33	4.2740	0.2340	72.7562	17.0229	0.0137
34	4.4664	0.2239	77.0302	17.2468	0.0130
35	4.6673	0.2143	81.4965	17.4610	0.0123
36	4.8774	0.2050	86.1639	17.6660	0.0116
37	5.0969	0.1962	91.0412	17.8622	0.0110
38	5.3262	0.1878	96.1381	18.0500	0.0104
39	5.5659	0.1797	101.4643	18.2297	0.0099
40	5.8164	0.1719	107.0302	18.4016	0.0093
41	6.0781	0.1645	112.8466	18.5661	0.0089
42	6.3516	0.1574	118.9247	18.7235	0.0084
43	6.6374	0.1507	125.2763	18.8742	0.0080
44	6.9361	0.1442	131.9137	19.0184	0.0076
45	7.2482	0.1380	138.8498	19.1563	0.0072
46	7.5744	0.1320	146.0980	19.2884	0.0068
47	7.9153	0.1263	153.6724	19.4147	0.0065
48	8.2714	0.1209	161.5877	19.5356	0.0062
49	8.6437	0.1157	169.8592	19.6513	0.0059
50	9.0326	0.1107	178.5028	19.7620	0.0056

5%

PERIOD	COMPOUND INTEREST	PRESENT VALUE	AMOUNT OF ANNUITY	PRESENT VALUE OF ANNUITY	SINKING FUND
1	1.0500	0.9524	1.0000	0.9524	1.0000
2	1.1025	0.9070	2.0500	1.8594	0.4878
3	1.1576	0.8638	3.1525	2.7232	0.3172
4	1.2155	0.8227	4.3101	3.5459	0.2320
5	1.2763	0.7835	5.5256	4.3295	0.1810
6	1.3401	0.7462	6.8019	5.0757	0.1470
7	1.4071	0.7107	8.1420	5.7864	0.1228
8	1.4775	0.6768	9.5491	6.4632	0.1047
9	1.5513	0.6446	11.0265	7.1078	0.0907
10	1.6289	0.6139	12.5779	7.7217	0.0795
11	1.7103	0.5847	14.2068	8.3064	0.0704
12	1.7959	0.5568	15.9171	8.8632	0.0628
13	1.8856	0.5303	17.7129	9.3936	0.0565
14	1.9799	0.5051	19.5986	9.8986	0.0510
15	2.0789	0.4810	21.5785	10.3796	0.0463
16	2.1829	0.4581	23.6574	10.8378	0.0423
17	2.2920	0.4363	25.8403	11.2741	0.0387
18	2.4066	0.4155	28.1323	11.6896	0.0355
19	2.5270	0.3957	30.5389	12.0853	0.0327
20	2.6533	0.3769	33.0659	12.4622	0.0302
21	2.7860	0.3589	35.7192	12.8211	0.0280
22	2.9253	0.3418	38.5051	13.1630	0.0260
23	3.0715	0.3256	41.4304	13.4886	0.0241
24	3.2251	0.3101	44.5019	13.7986	0.0225
25	3.3864	0.2953	47.7270	14.0939	0.0210
26	3.5557	0.2812	51.1133	14.3752	0.0196
27	3.7335	0.2678	54.6690	14.6430	0.0183
28	3.9201	0.2551	58.4024	14.8981	0.0171
29	4.1161	0.2429	62.3225	15.1411	0.0160
30	4.3219	0.2314	66.4386	15.3724	0.0151
31	4.5380	0.2204	70.7606	15.5928	0.0141
32	4.7649	0.2099	75.2986	15.8027	0.0133
33	5.0032	0.1999	80.0635	16.0025	0.0125
34	5.2533	0.1904	85.0667	16.1929	0.0118
35	5.5160	0.1813	90.3200	16.3742	0.0111
36	5.7918	0.1727	95.8360	16.5468	0.0104
37	6.0814	0.1644	101.6278	16.7113	0.0098
38	6.3855	0.1566	107.7092	16.8679	0.0093
39	6.7047	0.1491	114.0946	17.0170	0.0088
40	7.0400	0.1420	120.7993	17.1591	0.0083
41	7.3920	0.1353	127.8393	17.2944	0.0078
42	7.7616	0.1288	135.2312	17.4232	0.0074
43	8.1496	0.1227	142.9928	17.5459	0.0070
44	8.5571	0.1169	151.1424	17.6628	0.0066
45	8.9850	0.1113	159.6995	17.7741	0.0063
46	9.4342	0.1060	168.6845	17.8801	0.0059
47	9.9059	0.1009	178.1187	17.9810	0.0056
48	10.4012	0.0961	188.0246	18.0772	0.0053
49	10.9213	0.0916	198.4258	18.1687	0.0050
50	11.4674	0.0872	209.3470	18.2559	0.0048

PERIOD	COMPOUND INTEREST	PRESENT VALUE	AMOUNT OF ANNUITY	PRESENT VALUE OF ANNUITY	SINKING FUND
1	1.0550	0.9479	1.0000	0.9479	1.0000
2	1.1130	0.8985	2.0550	1.8463	0.4866
3	1.1742	0.8516	3.1680	2.6979	0.3157
4	1.2388	0.8072	4.3423	3.5051	0.2303
5	1.3070	0.7651	5.5811	4.2703	0.1792
6	1.3788	0.7252	6.8880	4.9955	0.1452
7	1.4547	0.6874	8.2669	5.6830	0.1210
8	1.5347	0.6516	9.7216	6.3346	0.1029
9	1.6191	0.6176	11.2562	6.9522	0.0888
10	1.7081	0.5854	12.8753	7.5376	0.0777
11	1.8021	0.5549	14.5835	8.0925	0.0686
12	1.9012	0.5260	16.3856	8.6185	0.0610
13	2.0058	0.4986	18.2868	9.1171	0.0547
14	2.1161	0.4726	20.2925	9.5896	0.0493
15	2.2325	0.4479	22.4086	10.0376	0.0446
16	2.3553	0.4246	24.6411	10.4622	0.0406
17	2.4848	0.4024	26.9963	10.8646	0.0370
18	2.6215	0.3815	29.4811	11.2461	0.0339
19	2.7656	0.3616	32.1026	11.6076	0.0312
20	2.9178	0.3427	34.8682	11.9504	0.0287
21	3.0782	0.3249	37.7860	12.2752	0.0265
22	3.2475	0.3079	40.8642	12.5832	0.0245
23	3.4261	0.2919	44.1117	12.8750	0.0227
24	3.6146	0.2767	47.5379	13.1517	0.0210
25	3.8134	0.2622	51.1524	13.4139	0.0195
26	4.0231	0.2486	54.9658	13.6625	0.0182
27	4.2444	0.2356	58.9889	13.8981	0.0170
28	4.4778	0.2233	63.2333	14.1214	0.0158
29	4.7241	0.2117	67.7112	14.3331	0.0148
30	4.9839	0.2006	72.4353	14.5337	0.0138
31	5.2581	0.1902	77.4192	14.7239	0.0129
32	5.5472	0.1803	82.6772	14.9042	0.0121
33	5.8523	0.1709	88.2245	15.0751	0.0113
34	6.1742	0.1620	94.0768	15.2370	0.0106
35	6.5138	0.1535	100.2510	15.3905	0.0100
36	6.8721	0.1455	106.7648	15.5361	0.0094
37	7.2500	0.1379	113.6369	15.6740	0.0088
38	7.6488	0.1307	120.8869	15.8047	0.0083
39	8.0695	0.1239	128.5357	15.9287	0.0078
40	8.5133	0.1175	136.6051	16.0461	0.0073
41	8.9815	0.1113	145.1184	16.1575	0.0069
42	9.4755	0.1055	154.0999	16.2630	0.0065
43	9.9966	0.1000	163.5753	16.3630	0.0061
44	10.5465	0.0948	173.5720	16.4578	0.0058
45	11.1265	0.0899	184.1184	16.5477	0.0054
46	11.7385	0.0852	195.2449	16.6329	0.0051
47	12.3841	0.0807	206.9834	16.7137	0.0048
48	13.0652	0.0765	219.3674	16.7902	0.0046
49	13.7838	0.0725	232.4326	16.8627	0.0043
50	14.5419	0.0688	246.2164	16.9315	0.0041

6%

PERIOD	COMPOUND INTEREST	PRESENT VALUE	AMOUNT OF ANNUITY	PRESENT VALUE OF ANNUITY	SINKING FUND
1	1.0600	0.9434	1.0000	0.9434	1.0000
2	1.1236	0.8900	2.0600	1.8334	0.4854
3	1.1910	0.8396	3.1836	2.6730	0.3141
4	1.2625	0.7921	4.3746	3.4651	0.2286
5	1.3382	0.7473	5.6371	4.2124	0.1774
6	1.4185	0.7050	6.9753	4.9173	0.1434
7	1.5036	0.6651	8.3938	5.5824	0.1191
8	1.5938	0.6274	9.8975	6.2098	0.1010
9	1.6895	0.5919	11.4913	6.8017	0.0870
10	1.7908	0.5584	13.1808	7.3601	0.0759
11	1.8983	0.5268	14.9716	7.8869	0.0668
12	2.0122	0.4970	16.8699	8.3838	0.0593
13	2.1329	0.4688	18.8821	8.8527	0.0530
14	2.2609	0.4423	21.0150	9.2950	0.0476
15	2.3966	0.4173	23.2759	9.7122	0.0430
16	2.5404	0.3936	25.6725	10.1059	0.0390
17	2.6928	0.3714	28.2128	10.4773	0.0354
18	2.8543	0.3503	30.9056	10.8276	0.0324
19	3.0256	0.3305	33.7599	11.1581	0.0296
20	3.2071	0.3118	36.7855	11.4699	0.0272
21	3.3996	0.2942	39.9927	11.7641	0.0250
22	3.6035	0.2775	43.3922	12.0416	0.0230
23	3.8197	0.2618	46.9958	12.3034	0.0213
24	4.0489	0.2470	50.8155	12.5504	0.0197
25	4.2919	0.2330	54.8644	12.7834	0.0182
26	4.5494	0.2198	59.1563	13.0032	0.0169
27	4.8223	0.2074	63.7057	13.2105	0.0157
28	5.1117	0.1956	68.5280	13.4062	0.0146
29	5.4184	0.1846	73.6397	13.5907	0.0136
30	5.7435	0.1741	79.0580	13.7648	0.0126
31	6.0881	0.1643	84.8015	13.9291	0.0118
32	6.4534	0.1550	90.8896	14.0840	0.0110
33	6.8406	0.1462	97.3430	14.2302	0.0103
34	7.2510	0.1379	104.1836	14.3681	0.0096
35	7.6861	0.1301	111.4346	14.4982	0.0090
36	8.1472	0.1227	119.1206	14.6210	0.0084
37	8.6361	0.1158	127.2679	14.7368	0.0079
38	9.1542	0.1092	135.9039	14.8460	0.0074
39	9.7035	0.1031	145.0581	14.9491	0.0069
40	10.2857	0.0972	154.7616	15.0463	0.0065
41	10.9028	0.0917	165.0473	15.1380	0.0061
42	11.5570	0.0865	175.9501	15.2245	0.0057
43	12.2504	0.0816	187.5071	15.3062	0.0053
44	12.9855	0.0770	199.7575	15.3832	0.0050
45	13.7646	0.0727	212.7430	15.4558	0.0047
46	14.5905	0.0685	226.5076	15.5244	0.0044
47	15.4659	0.0647	241.0980	15.5890	0.0041
48	16.3938	0.0610	256.5639	15.6500	0.0039
49	17.3775	0.0575	272.9577	15.7076	0.0037
50	18.4201	0.0543	290.3351	15.7619	0.0034

PERIOD	COMPOUND INTEREST	PRESENT VALUE	AMOUNT OF ANNUITY	PRESENT VALUE OF ANNUITY	SINKING FUND
1	1.0650	0.9390	1.0000	0.9390	1.0000
2	1.1342	0.8817	2.0650	1.8206	0.4843
3	1.2079	0.8278	3.1992	2.6485	0.3126
4	1.2865	0.7773	4.4072	3.4258	0.2269
5	1.3701	0.7299	5.6936	4.1557	0.1756
6	1.4591	0.6853	7.0637	4.8410	0.1416
7	1.5540	0.6435	8.5229	5.4845	0.1173
8	1.6550	0.6042	10.0768	6.0887	0.0992
9	1.7626	0.5674	11.7318	6.6561	0.0852
10	1.8771	0.5327	13.4944	7.1888	0.0741
11	1.9992	0.5002	15.3715	7.6890	0.0651
12	2.1291	0.4697	17.3707	8.1587	0.0576
13	2.2675	0.4410	19.4998	8.5997	0.0513
14	2.4149	0.4141	21.7673	9.0138	0.0459
15	2.5718	0.3888	24.1821	9.4027	0.0414
16	2.7390	0.3651	26.7540	9.7678	0.0374
17	2.9170	0.3428	29.4930	10.1106	0.0339
18	3.1067	0.3219	32.4100	10.4325	0.0309
19	3.3086	0.3022	35.5167	10.7347	0.0282
20	3.5236	0.2838	38.8253	11.0185	0.0258
21	3.7527	0.2665	42.3489	11.2850	0.0236
22	3.9966	0.2502	46.1016	11.5352	0.0217
23	4.2564	0.2349	50.0982	11.7701	0.0200
24	4.5330	0.2206	54.3546	11.9907	0.0184
25	4.8277	0.2071	58.8876	12.1979	0.0170
26	5.1415	0.1945	63.7153	12.3924	0.0157
27	5.4757	0.1826	68.8568	12.5750	0.0145
28	5.8316	0.1715	74.3325	12.7465	0.0135
29	6.2107	0.1610	80.1641	12.9075	0.0125
30	6.6144	0.1512	86.3747	13.0587	0.0116
31	7.0443	0.1420	92.9891	13.2006	0.0108
32	7.5022	0.1333	100.0334	13.3339	0.0100
33	7.9898	0.1252	107.5355	13.4591	0.0093
34	8.5091	0.1175	115.5254	13.5766	0.0087
35	9.0622	0.1103	124.0345	13.6870	0.0081
36	9.6513	0.1036	133.0967	13.7906	0.0075
37	10.2786	0.0973	142.7480	13.8879	0.0070
38	10.9467	0.0914	153.0266	13.9792	0.0065
39	11.6583	0.0858	163.9733	14.0650	0.0061
40	12.4161	0.0805	175.6316	14.1455	0.0057
41	13.2231	0.0756	188.0476	14.2212	0.0053
42	14.0826	0.0710	201.2707	14.2922	0.0050
43	14.9980	0.0667	215.3533	14.3588	0.0046
44	15.9728	0.0626	230.3513	14.4214	0.0043
45	17.0111	0.0588	246.3241	14.4802	0.0041
46	18.1168	0.0552	263.3352	14.5354	0.0038
47	19.2944	0.0518	281.4519	14.5873	0.0036
48	20.5485	0.0487	300.7463	14.6359	0.0033
49	21.8842	0.0457	321.2948	14.6816	0.0031
50	23.3066	0.0429	343.1789	14.7245	0.0029

7%

PERIOD	COMPOUND INTEREST	PRESENT VALUE	AMOUNT OF ANNUITY	PRESENT VALUE OF ANNUITY	SINKING FUND
1	1.0700	0.9346	1.0000	0.9346	1.0000
2	1.1449	0.8734	2.0700	1.8080	0.4831
3	1.2250	0.8163	3.2149	2.6243	0.3111
4	1.3108	0.7629	4.4399	3.3872	0.2252
5	1.4026	0.7130	5.7507	4.1002	0.1739
6	1.5007	0.6663	7.1533	4.7665	0.1398
7	1.6058	0.6227	8.6540	5.3893	0.1156
8	1.7182	0.5820	10.2598	5.9713	0.0975
9	1.8385	0.5439	11.9780	6.5152	0.0835
10	1.9672	0.5083	13.8164	7.0236	0.0724
11	2.1049	0.4751	15.7836	7.4987	0.0634
12	2.2522	0.4440	17.8884	7.9427	0.0559
13	2.4098	0.4150	20.1406	8.3576	0.0497
14	2.5785	0.3878	22.5505	8.7455	0.0443
15	2.7590	0.3624	25.1290	9.1079	0.0398
16	2.9522	0.3387	27.8880	9.4466	0.0359
17	3.1588	0.3166	30.8402	9.7632	0.0324
18	3.3799	0.2959	33.9990	10.0591	0.0294
19	3.6165	0.2765	37.3789	10.3356	0.0268
20	3.8697	0.2584	40.9954	10.5940	0.0244
21	4.1406	0.2415	44.8651	10.8355	0.0223
22	4.4304	0.2257	49.0057	11.0612	0.0204
23	4.7405	0.2109	53.4360	11.2722	0.0187
24	5.0724	0.1971	58.1766	11.4693	0.0172
25	5.4274	0.1842	63.2489	11.6536	0.0158
26	5.8074	0.1722	68.6763	11.8258	0.0146
27	6.2139	0.1609	74.4837	11.9867	0.0134
28	6.6488	0.1504	80.6975	12.1371	0.0124
29	7.1143	0.1406	87.3464	12.2777	0.0114
30	7.6123	0.1314	94.4606	12.4090	0.0106
31	8.1451	0.1228	102.0728	12.5318	0.0098
32	8.7153	0.1147	110.2179	12.6466	0.0091
33	9.3253	0.1072	118.9332	12.7538	0.0084
34	9.9781	0.1002	128.2585	12.8540	0.0078
35	10.6766	0.0937	138.2366	12.9477	0.0072
36	11.4239	0.0875	148.9131	13.0352	0.0067
37	12.2236	0.0818	160.3370	13.1170	0.0062
38	13.0792	0.0765	172.5606	13.1935	0.0058
39	13.9948	0.0715	185.6398	13.2649	0.0054
40	14.9744	0.0668	199.6346	13.3317	0.0050
41	16.0226	0.0624	214.6090	13.3941	0.0047
42	17.1442	0.0583	230.6317	13.4524	0.0043
43	18.3443	0.0545	247.7758	13.5070	0.0040
44	19.6284	0.0509	266.1201	13.5579	0.0038
45	21.0024	0.0476	285.7485	13.6055	0.0035
46	22.4726	0.0445	306.7509	13.6500	0.0033
47	24.0456	0.0416	329.2234	13.6916	0.0030
48	25.7288	0.0389	353.2691	13.7305	0.0028
49	27.5298	0.0363	378.9978	13.7668	0.0026
50	29.4569	0.0339	406.5277	13.8007	0.0025

PERIOD	COMPOUND INTEREST	PRESENT VALUE	AMOUNT OF ANNUITY	PRESENT VALUE OF ANNUITY	SINKING FUND
1	1.0750	0.9302	1.0000	0.9302	1.0000
2	1.1556	0.8653	2.0750	1.7956	0.4819
3	1.2423	0.8050	3.2306	2.6005	0.3095
4	1.3355	0.7488	4.4729	3.3493	0.2236
5	1.4356	0.6966	5.8084	4.0459	0.1722
6	1.5433	0.6480	7.2440	4.6938	0.1380
7	1.6590	0.6028	8.7873	5.2966	0.1138
8	1.7835	0.5607	10.4464	5.8573	0.0957
9	1.9172	0.5216	12.2299	6.3789	0.0818
10	2.0610	0.4852	14.1471	6.8641	0.0707
11	2.2156	0.4513	16.2081	7.3154	0.0617
12	2.3818	0.4199	18.4237	7.7353	0.0543
13	2.5604	0.3906	20.8055	8.1258	0.0481
14	2.7524	0.3633	23.3659	8.4892	0.0428
15	2.9589	0.3380	26.1184	8.8271	0.0383
16	3.1808	0.3144	29.0773	9.1415	0.0344
17	3.4194	0.2925	32.2581	9.4340	0.0310
18	3.6758	0.2720	35.6774	9.7060	0.0280
19	3.9515	0.2531	39.3532	9.9591	0.0254
20	4.2479	0.2354	43.3047	10.1945	0.0231
21	4.5664	0.2190	47.5526	10.4135	0.0210
22	4.9089	0.2037	52.1190	10.6172	0.0192
23	5.2771	0.1895	57.0280	10.8067	0.0175
24	5.6729	0.1763	62.3051	10.9830	0.0161
25	6.0983	0.1640	67.9780	11.1469	0.0147
26	6.5557	0.1525	74.0763	11.2995	0.0135
27	7.0474	0.1419	80.6320	11.4414	0.0124
28	7.5760	0.1320	87.6794	11.5734	0.0114
29	8.1442	0.1228	95.2554	11.6962	0.0105
30	8.7550	0.1142	103.3996	11.8104	0.0097
31	9.4116	0.1063	112.1545	11.9166	0.0089
32	10.1175	0.0988	121.5661	12.0155	0.0082
33	10.8763	0.0919	131.6836	12.1074	0.0076
34	11.6920	0.0855	142.5599	12.1930	0.0070
35	12.5689	0.0796	154.2519	12.2725	0.0065
36	13.5116	0.0740	166.8208	12.3465	0.0060
37	14.5249	0.0688	180.3323	12.4154	0.0055
38	15.6143	0.0640	194.8573	12.4794	0.0051
39	16.7854	0.0596	210.4716	12.5390	0.0048
40	18.0443	0.0554	227.2569	12.5944	0.0044
41	19.3976	0.0516	245.3012	12.6460	0.0041
42	20.8524	0.0480	264.6988	12.6939	0.0038
43	22.4163	0.0446	285.5513	12.7385	0.0035
44	24.0976	0.0415	307.9676	12.7800	0.0032
45	25.9049	0.0386	332.0652	12.8186	0.0030
46	27.8478	0.0359	357.9701	12.8545	0.0028
47	29.9363	0.0334	385.8179	12.8879	0.0026
48	32.1816	0.0311	415.7542	12.9190	0.0024
49	34.5952	0.0289	447.9358	12.9479	0.0022
50	37.1898	0.0269	482.5310	12.9748	0.0021

8%

PERIOD	COMPOUND INTEREST	PRESENT VALUE	AMOUNT OF ANNUITY	PRESENT VALUE OF ANNUITY	SINKING FUND
1	1.0800	0.9259	1.0000	0.9259	1.0000
2	1.1664	0.8573	2.0800	1.7833	0.4808
3	1.2597	0.7938	3.2464	2.5771	0.3080
4	1.3605	0.7350	4.5061	3.3121	0.2219
5	1.4693	0.6806	5.8666	3.9927	0.1705
6	1.5869	0.6302	7.3359	4.6229	0.1363
7	1.7138	0.5835	8.9228	5.2064	0.1121
8	1.8509	0.5403	10.6366	5.7466	0.0940
9	1.9990	0.5002	12.4876	6.2469	0.0801
10	2.1589	0.4632	14.4866	6.7101	0.0690
11	2.3316	0.4289	16.6455	7.1390	0.0601
12	2.5182	0.3971	18.9771	7.5361	0.0527
13	2.7196	0.3677	21.4953	7.9038	0.0465
14	2.9372	0.3405	24.2149	8.2442	0.0413
15	3.1722	0.3152	27.1521	8.5595	0.0368
16	3.4259	0.2919	30.3243	8.8514	0.0330
17	3.7000	0.2703	33.7503	9.1216	0.0296
18	3.9960	0.2502	37.4503	9.3719	0.0267
19	4.3157	0.2317	41.4463	9.6036	0.0241
20	4.6610	0.2145	45.7620	9.8181	0.0219
21	5.0338	0.1987	50.4230	10.0168	0.0198
22	5.4365	0.1839	55.4568	10.2007	0.0180
23	5.8715	0.1703	60.8933	10.3711	0.0164
24	6.3412	0.1577	66.7648	10.5288	0.0150
25	6.8485	0.1460	73.1060	10.6748	0.0137
26	7.3964	0.1352	79.9545	10.8100	0.0125
27	7.9881	0.1252	87.3509	10.9352	0.0114
28	8.6271	0.1159	95.3389	11.0511	0.0105
29	9.3173	0.1073	103.9660	11.1584	0.0096
30	10.0627	0.0994	113.2833	11.2578	0.0088
31	10.8677	0.0920	123.3460	11.3498	0.0081
32	11.7371	0.0852	134.2137	11.4350	0.0075
33	12.6761	0.0789	145.9508	11.5139	0.0069
34	13.6901	0.0730	158.6269	11.5869	0.0063
35	14.7854	0.0676	172.3170	11.6546	0.0058
36	15.9682	0.0626	187.1024	11.7172	0.0053
37	17.2456	0.0580	203.0706	11.7752	0.0049
38	18.6253	0.0537	220.3162	11.8289	0.0045
39	20.1153	0.0497	238.9415	11.8786	0.0042
40	21.7245	0.0460	259.0569	11.9246	0.0039
41	23.4625	0.0426	280.7814	11.9672	0.0036
42	25.3395	0.0395	304.2440	12.0067	0.0033
43	27.3667	0.0365	329.5835	12.0432	0.0030
44	29.5560	0.0338	356.9502	12.0771	0.0028
45	31.9205	0.0313	386.5062	12.1084	0.0026
46	34.4741	0.0290	418.4267	12.1374	0.0024
47	37.2321	0.0269	452.9009	12.1643	0.0022
48	40.2106	0.0249	490.1329	12.1891	0.0020
49	43.4275	0.0230	530.3436	12.2122	0.0019
50	46.9017	0.0213	573.7711	12.2335	0.0017

PERIOD	COMPOUND INTEREST	PRESENT VALUE	AMOUNT OF ANNUITY	PRESENT VALUE OF ANNUITY	SINKING FUND
1	1.0850	0.9217	1.0000	0.9217	1.0000
2	1.1772	0.8495	2.0850	1.7711	0.4796
3	1.2773	0.7829	3.2622	2.5540	0.3065
4	1.3859	0.7216	4.5395	3.2756	0.2203
5	1.5037	0.6650	5.9254	3.9406	0.1688
6	1.6315	0.6129	7.4290	4.5536	0.1346
7	1.7701	0.5649	9.0605	5.1185	0.1104
8	1.9206	0.5207	10.8307	5.6392	0.0923
9	2.0839	0.4799	12.7513	6.1191	0.0784
10	2.2610	0.4423	14.8351	6.5614	0.0674
11	2.4532	0.4076	17.0961	6.9690	0.0585
12	2.6617	0.3757	19.5493	7.3447	0.0512
13	2.8879	0.3463	22.2110	7.6910	0.0450
14	3.1334	0.3191	25.0989	8.0101	0.0398
15	3.3997	0.2941	28.2323	8.3042	0.0354
16	3.6887	0.2711	31.6321	8.5753	0.0316
17	4.0023	0.2499	35.3208	8.8252	0.0283
18	4.3425	0.2303	39.3230	9.0555	0.0254
19	4.7116	0.2122	43.6655	9.2677	0.0229
20	5.1121	0.1956	48.3771	9.4633	0.0207
21	5.5466	0.1803	53.4891	9.6436	0.0187
22	6.0180	0.1662	59.0357	9.8098	0.0169
23	6.5296	0.1531	65.0538	9.9629	0.0154
24	7.0846	0.1412	71.5833	10.1041	0.0140
25	7.6868	0.1301	78.6679	10.2342	0.0127
26	8.3401	0.1199	86.3547	10.3541	0.0116
27	9.0491	0.1105	94.6949	10.4646	0.0106
28	9.8182	0.1019	103.7439	10.5665	0.0096
29	10.6528	0.0939	113.5622	10.6603	0.0088
30	11.5583	0.0865	124.2149	10.7468	0.0081
31	12.5407	0.0797	135.7732	10.8266	0.0074
32	13.6067	0.0735	148.3140	10.9001	0.0067
33	14.7633	0.0677	161.9207	10.9678	0.0062
34	16.0181	0.0624	176.6839	11.0302	0.0057
35	17.3797	0.0575	192.7021	11.0878	0.0052
36	18.8569	0.0530	210.0818	11.1408	0.0048
37	20.4598	0.0489	228.9387	11.1897	0.0044
38	22.1989	0.0450	249.3985	11.2347	0.0040
39	24.0858	0.0415	271.5974	11.2763	0.0037
40	26.1331	0.0383	295.6832	11.3145	0.0034
41	28.3544	0.0353	321.8163	11.3498	0.0031
42	30.7645	0.0325	350.1707	11.3823	0.0029
43	33.3795	0.0300	380.9352	11.4123	0.0026
44	36.2168	0.0276	414.3148	11.4399	0.0024
45	39.2952	0.0254	450.5315	11.4653	0.0022
46	42.6353	0.0235	489.8267	11.4888	0.0020
47	46.2593	0.0216	532.4620	11.5104	0.0019
48	50.1913	0.0199	578.7213	11.5303	0.0017
49	54.4576	0.0184	628.9127	11.5487	0.0016
50	59.0865	0.0169	683.3703	11.5656	0.0015

9%

PERIOD	COMPOUND INTEREST	PRESENT VALUE	AMOUNT OF ANNUITY	PRESENT VALUE OF ANNUITY	SINKING FUND
1	1.0900	0.9174	1.0000	0.9174	1.0000
2	1.1881	0.8417	2.0900	1.7591	0.4785
3	1.2950	0.7722	3.2781	2.5313	0.3051
4	1.4116	0.7084	4.5731	3.2397	0.2187
5	1.5386	0.6499	5.9847	3.8897	0.1671
6	1.6771	0.5963	7.5233	4.4859	0.1329
7	1.8280	0.5470	9.2004	5.0330	0.1087
8	1.9926	0.5019	11.0285	5.5348	0.0907
9	2.1719	0.4604	13.0210	5.9952	0.0768
10	2.3674	0.4224	15.1929	6.4177	0.0658
11	2.5804	0.3875	17.5603	6.8052	0.0569
12	2.8127	0.3555	20.1407	7.1607	0.0497
13	3.0658	0.3262	22.9534	7.4869	0.0436
14	3.3417	0.2992	26.0192	7.7862	0.0384
15	3.6425	0.2745	29.3609	8.0607	0.0341
16	3.9703	0.2519	33.0034	8.3126	0.0303
17	4.3276	0.2311	36.9737	8.5436	0.0270
18	4.7171	0.2120	41.3014	8.7556	0.0242
19	5.1417	0.1945	46.0185	8.9501	0.0217
20	5.6044	0.1784	51.1602	9.1285	0.0195
21	6.1088	0.1637	56.7646	9.2922	0.0176
22	6.6586	0.1502	62.8734	9.4424	0.0159
23	7.2579	0.1378	69.5320	9.5802	0.0144
24	7.9111	0.1264	76.7899	9.7066	0.0130
25	3.6231	0.1160	84.7010	9.8226	0.0118
26	9.3992	0.1064	93.3241	9.9290	0.0107
27	10.2451	0.0976	102.7233	10.0266	0.0097
28	11.1672	0.0895	112.9684	10.1161	0.0089
29	12.1722	0.0822	124.1355	10.1983	0.0081
30	13.2677	0.0754	136.3077	10.2737	0.0073
31	14.4618	0.0691	149.5754	10.3428	0.0067
32	15.7634	0.0634	164.0372	10.4062	0.0061
33	17.1821	0.0582	179.8006	10.4644	0.0056
34	18.7284	0.0534	196.9827	10.5178	0.0051
35	20.4140	0.0490	215.7111	10.5668	0.0046
36	22.2513	0.0449	236.1251	10.6118	0.0042
37	24.2539	0.0412	258.3764	10.6530	0.0039
38	26.4367	0.0378	282.6303	10.6908	0.0035
39	28.8160	0.0347	309.0670	10.7255	0.0032
40	31.4095	0.0318	337.8831	10.7574	0.0030
41	34.2363	0.0292	369.2925	10.7866	0.0027
42	37.3176	0.0268	403.5289	10.8134	0.0025
43	40.6762	0.0246	440.8465	10.8380	0.0023
44	44.3371	0.0226	481.5228	10.8605	0.0021
45	48.3274	0.0207	525.8598	10.8812	0.0019
46	52.6769	0.0190	574.1872	10.9002	0.0017
47	57.4178	0.0174	626.8641	10.9176	0.0016
48	62.5854	0.0160	684.2819	10.9336	0.0015
49	68.2181	0.0147	746.8673	10.9482	0.0013
50	74.3577	0.0134	815.0853	10.9617	0.0012

PERIOD	COMPOUND INTEREST	PRESENT VALUE	AMOUNT OF ANNUITY	PRESENT VALUE OF ANNUITY	SINKING FUND
1	1.0950	0.9132	1.0000	0.9132	1.0000
2	1.1990	0.8340	2.0950	1.7473	0.4773
3	1.3129	0.7617	3.2940	2.5089	0.3036
4	1.4377	0.6956	4.6070	3.2045	0.2171
5	1.5742	0.6352	6.0446	3.8397	0.1654
6	1.7238	0.5801	7.6189	4.4198	0.1313
7	1.8876	0.5298	9.3427	4.9496	0.1070
8	2.0669	0.4838	11.2302	5.4334	0.0890
9	2.2632	0.4418	13.2971	5.8753	0.0752
10	2.4782	0.4035	15.5603	6.2788	0.0643
11	2.7137	0.3685	18.0385	6.6473	0.0554
12	2.9715	0.3365	20.7522	6.9838	0.0482
13	3.2537	0.3073	23.7236	7.2912	0.0422
14	3.5629	0.2807	26.9774	7.5719	0.0371
15	3.9013	0.2563	30.5402	7.8282	0.0327
16	4.2719	0.2341	34.4416	8.0623	0.0290
17	4.6778	0.2138	38.7135	8.2760	0.0258
18	5.1222	0.1952	43.3913	8.4713	0.0230
19	5.6088	0.1783	48.5135	8.6496	0.0206
20	6.1416	0.1628	54.1223	8.8124	0.0185
21	6.7251	0.1487	60.2639	8.9611	0.0166
22	7.3639	0.1358	66.9889	9.0969	0.0149
23	8.0635	0.1240	74.3529	9.2209	0.0134
24	8.8296	0.1133	82.4164	9.3341	0.0121
25	9.6684	0.1034	91.2460	9.4376	0.0110
26	10.5869	0.0945	100.9143	9.5320	0.0099
27	11.5926	0.0863	111.5012	9.6183	0.0090
28	12.6939	0.0788	123.0938	9.6971	0.0081
29	13.8998	0.0719	135.7877	9.7690	0.0074
30	15.2203	0.0657	149.6876	9.8347	0.0067
31	16.6663	0.0600	164.9079	9.8947	0.0061
32	18.2495	0.0548	181.5741	9.9495	0.0055
33	19.9833	0.0500	199.8237	9.9996	0.0050
34	21.8817	0.0457	219.8069	10.0453	0.0045
35	23.9604	0.0417	241.6886	10.0870	0.0041
36	26.2367	0.0381	265.6490	10.1251	0.0038
37	28.7291	0.0348	291.8857	10.1599	0.0034
38	31.4584	0.0318	320.6148	10.1917	0.0031
39	34.4470	0.0290	352.0732	10.2207	0.0028
40	37.7194	0.0265	386.5202	10.2472	0.0026
41	41.3028	0.0242	424.2396	10.2715	0.0024
42	45.2265	0.0221	465.5424	10.2936	0.0021
43	49.5231	0.0202	510.7689	10.3138	0.0020
44	54.2277	0.0184	560.2920	10.3322	0.0018
45	59.3794	0.0168	614.5197	10.3490	0.0016
46	65.0204	0.0154	673.8991	10.3644	0.0015
47	71.1974	0.0140	738.9195	10.3785	0.0014
48	77.9611	0.0128	810.1168	10.3913	0.0012
49	85.3674	0.0117	888.0779	10.4030	0.0011
50	93.4773	0.0107	973.4453	10.4137	0.0010

10%

PERIOD	COMPOUND INTEREST	PRESENT VALUE	AMOUNT OF ANNUITY	PRESENT VALUE OF ANNUITY	SINKING FUND
1	1.1000	0.9091	1.0000	0.9091	1.0000
2	1.2100	0.8264	2.1000	1.7355	0.4762
3	1.3310	0.7513	3.3100	2.4869	0.3021
4	1.4641	0.6830	4.6410	3.1699	0.2155
5	1.6105	0.6209	6.1051	3.7908	0.1638
6	1.7716	0.5645	7.7156	4.3553	0.1296
7	1.9487	0.5132	9.4872	4.8684	0.1054
8	2.1436	0.4665	11.4359	5.3349	0.0874
9	2.3579	0.4241	13.5795	5.7590	0.0736
10	2.5937	0.3855	15.9374	6.1446	0.0627
11	2.8531	0.3505	18.5312	6.4951	0.0540
12	3.1384	0.3186	21.3843	6.8137	0.0468
13	3.4523	0.2897	24.5227	7.1034	0.0408
14	3.7975	0.2633	27.9750	7.3667	0.0357
15	4.1772	0.2394	31.7725	7.6061	0.0315
16	4.5950	0.2176	35.9497	7.8237	0.0278
17	5.0545	0.1978	40.5447	8.0216	0.0247
18	5.5599	0.1799	45.5992	8.2014	0.0219
19	6.1159	0.1635	51.1591	8.3649	0.0195
20	6.7275	0.1486	57.2750	8.5136	0.0175
21	7.4002	0.1351	64.0025	8.6487	0.0156
22	8.1403	0.1228	71.4028	8.7715	0.0140
23	8.9543	0.1117	79.5430	8.8832	0.0126
24	9.8497	0.1015	88.4974	8.9847	0.0113
25	10.8347	0.0923	98.3471	9.0770	0.0102
26	11.9182	0.0839	109.1818	9.1609	0.0092
27	13.1100	0.0763	121.1000	9.2372	0.0083
28	14.4210	0.0693	134.2100	9.3066	0.0075
29	15.8631	0.0630	148.6310	9.3696	0.0067
30	17.4494	0.0573	164.4941	9.4269	0.0061
31	19.1944	0.0521	181.9435	9.4790	0.0055
32	21.1138	0.0474	201.1379	9.5264	0.0050
33	23.2252	0.0431	222.2517	9.5694	0.0045
34	25.5477	0.0391	245.4768	9.6086	0.0041
35	28.1025	0.0356	271.0245	9.6442	0.0037
36	30.9127	0.0323	299.1270	9.6765	0.0033
37	34.0040	0.0294	330.0397	9.7059	0.0030
38	37.4044	0.0267	364.0436	9.7327	0.0027
39	41.1448	0.0243	401.4480	9.7570	0.0025
40	45.2593	0.0221	442.5928	9.7790	0.0023
41	49.7852	0.0201	487.8520	9.7991	0.0020
42	54.7637	0.0183	537.6373	9.8174	0.0019
43	60.2401	0.0166	592.4010	9.8340	0.0017
44	66.2641	0.0151	652.6411	9.8491	0.0015
45	72.8905	0.0137	718.9052	9.8628	0.0014
46	80.1796	0.0125	791.7957	9.8753	0.0013
47	88.1975	0.0113	871.9753	9.8866	0.0011
48	97.0173	0.0103	960.1730	9.8969	0.0010
49	106.7190	0.0094	1057.1900	9.9063	0.0009
50	117.3909	0.0085	1163.9090	9.9148	0.0009

PERIOD	COMPOUND INTEREST	PRESENT VALUE	AMOUNT OF ANNUITY	PRESENT VALUE OF ANNUITY	SINKING FUND
1	1.1050	0.9050	1.0000	0.9050	1.0000
2	1.2210	0.8190	2.1050	1.7240	0.4751
3	1.3492	0.7412	3.3260	2.4651	0.3007
4	1.4909	0.6707	4.6753	3.1359	0.2139
5	1.6474	0.6070	6.1662	3.7429	0.1622
6	1.8204	0.5493	7.8136	4.2922	0.1280
7	2.0116	0.4971	9.6340	4.7893	0.1038
8	2.2228	0.4499	11.6456	5.2392	0.0859
9	2.4562	0.4071	13.8684	5.6463	0.0721
10	2.7141	0.3684	16.3246	6.0148	0.0613
11	2.9991	0.3334	19.0387	6.3482	0.0525
12	3.3140	0.3018	22.0377	6.6500	0.0454
13	3.6619	0.2731	25.3517	6.9230	0.0394
14	4.0464	0.2471	29.0136	7.1702	0.0345
15	4.4713	0.2236	33.0600	7.3938	0.0302
16	4.9408	0.2024	37.5313	7.5962	0.0266
17	5.4596	0.1832	42.4721	7.7794	0.0235
18	6.0328	0.1658	47.9317	7.9451	0.0209
19	6.6663	0.1500	53.9645	8.0952	0.0185
20	7.3662	0.1358	60.6308	8.2309	0.0165
21	8.1397	0.1229	67.9970	8.3538	0.0147
22	8.9944	0.1112	76.1367	8.4649	0.0131
23	9.9388	0.1006	85.1311	8.5656	0.0117
24	10.9823	0.0911	95.0699	8.6566	0.0105
25	12.1355	0.0824	106.0522	8.7390	0.0094
26	13.4097	0.0746	118.1877	8.8136	0.0085
27	14.8177	0.0675	131.5974	8.8811	0.0076
28	16.3736	0.0611	146.4151	8.9422	0.0068
29	18.0928	0.0553	162.7887	8.9974	0.0061
30	19.9926	0.0500	180.8815	9.0474	0.0055
31	22.0918	0.0453	200.8741	9.0927	0.0050
32	24.4114	0.0410	222.9659	9.1337	0.0045
33	26.9746	0.0371	247.3773	9.1707	0.0040
34	29.8070	0.0335	274.3519	9.2043	0.0036
35	32.9367	0.0304	304.1588	9.2347	0.0033
36	36.3950	0.0275	337.0955	9.2621	0.0030
37	40.2165	0.0249	373.4906	9.2870	0.0027
38	44.4392	0.0225	413.7070	9.3095	0.0024
39	49.1054	0.0204	458.1463	9.3299	0.0022
40	54.2614	0.0184	507.2517	9.3483	0.0020
41	59.9589	0.0167	561.5131	9.3650	0.0018
42	66.2546	0.0151	621.4720	9.3801	0.0016
43	73.2113	0.0137	687.7266	9.3937	0.0015
44	80.8985	0.0124	760.9378	9.4061	0.0013
45	89.3928	0.0112	841.8363	9.4173	0.0012
46	98.7791	0.0101	931.2291	9.4274	0.0011
47	109.1509	0.0092	1030.0080	9.4366	0.0010
48	120.6117	0.0083	1139.1590	9.4448	0.0009
49	133.2759	0.0075	1259.7710	9.4523	0.0008
50	147.2699	0.0068	1393.0470	9.4591	0.0007

11%

PERIOD	COMPOUND INTEREST	PRESENT VALUE	AMOUNT OF ANNUITY	PRESENT VALUE OF ANNUITY	SINKING FUND
1	1.1100	0.9009	1.0000	0.9009	1.0000
2	1.2321	0.8116	2.1100	1.7125	0.4739
3	1.3676	0.7312	3.3421	2.4437	0.2992
4	1.5181	0.6587	4.7097	3.1024	0.2123
5	1.6851	0.5935	6.2278	3.6959	0.1606
6	1.8704	0.5346	7.9129	4.2305	0.1264
7	2.0762	0.4817	9.7833	4.7122	0.1022
8	2.3045	0.4339	11.8594	5.1461	0.0843
9	2.5580	0.3909	14.1640	5.5370	0.0706
10	2.8394	0.3522	16.7220	5.8892	0.0598
11	3.1518	0.3173	19.5614	6.2065	0.0511
12	3.4985	0.2858	22.7132	6.4924	0.0440
13	3.8833	0.2575	26.2116	6.7499	0.0382
14	4.3104	0.2320	30.0949	6.9819	0.0332
15	4.7846	0.2090	34.4054	7.1909	0.0291
16	5.3109	0.1883	39.1899	7.3792	0.0255
17	5.8951	0.1696	44.5008	7.5488	0.0225
18	6.5436	0.1528	50.3959	7.7016	0.0198
19	7.2633	0.1377	56.9395	7.8393	0.0176
20	8.0623	0.1240	64.2028	7.9633	0.0156
21	8.9492	0.1117	72.2651	8.0751	0.0138
22	9.9336	0.1007	81.2143	8.1757	0.0123
23	11.0263	0.0907	91.1479	8.2664	0.0110
24	12.2392	0.0817	102.1741	8.3481	0.0098
25	13.5855	0.0736	114.4133	8.4217	0.0087
26	15.0799	0.0663	127.9988	8.4881	0.0078
27	16.7386	0.0597	143.0786	8.5478	0.0070
28	18.5799	0.0538	159.8173	8.6016	0.0063
29	20.6237	0.0485	178.3972	8.6501	0.0056
30	22.8923	0.0437	199.0209	8.6938	0.0050
31	25.4105	0.0394	221.9132	8.7331	0.0045
32	28.2056	0.0355	247.3236	8.7686	0.0040
33	31.3082	0.0319	275.5292	8.8005	0.0036
34	34.7521	0.0288	306.8374	8.8293	0.0033
35	38.5749	0.0259	341.5895	8.8552	0.0029
36	42.8181	0.0234	380.1644	8.8786	0.0026
37	47.5281	0.0210	422.9825	8.8996	0.0024
38	52.7562	0.0190	470.5106	8.9186	0.0021
39	58.5593	0.0171	523.2667	8.9357	0.0019
40	65.0009	0.0154	581.8260	8.9511	0.0017
41	72.1510	0.0139	646.8269	8.9649	0.0015
42	80.0876	0.0125	718.9779	8.9774	0.0014
43	88.8972	0.0112	799.0655	8.9886	0.0013
44	98.6759	0.0101	887.9626	8.9988	0.0011
45	109.5303	0.0091	986.6385	9.0079	0.0010
46	121.5786	0.0082	1096.1690	9.0161	0.0009
47	134.9522	0.0074	1217.7470	9.0235	0.0008
48	149.7970	0.0067	1352.7000	9.0302	0.0007
49	166.2746	0.0060	1502.4970	9.0362	0.0007
50	184.5649	0.0054	1668.7710	9.0417	0.0006

PERIOD	COMPOUND INTEREST	PRESENT VALUE	AMOUNT OF ANNUITY	PRESENT VALUE OF ANNUITY	SINKING FUND
1	1.1150	0.8969	1.0000	0.8969	1.0000
2	1.2432	0.8044	2.1150	1.7012	0.4728
3	1.3862	0.7214	3.3582	2.4226	0.2978
4	1.5456	0.6470	4.7444	3.0696	0.2108
5	1.7234	0.5803	6.2900	3.6499	0.1590
6	1.9215	0.5204	8.0134	4.1703	0.1248
7	2.1425	0.4667	9.9349	4.6370	0.1007
8	2.3889	0.4186	12.0774	5.0556	0.0828
9	2.6636	0.3754	14.4663	5.4311	0.0691
10	2.9699	0.3367	17.1300	5.7678	0.0584
11	3.3115	0.3020	20.0999	6.0697	0.0498
12	3.6923	0.2708	23.4114	6.3406	0.0427
13	4.1169	0.2429	27.1037	6.5835	0.0369
14	4.5904	0.2178	31.2206	6.8013	0.0320
15	5.1183	0.1954	35.8110	6.9967	0.0279
16	5.7069	0.1752	40.9293	7.1719	0.0244
17	6.3632	0.1572	46.6361	7.3291	0.0214
18	7.0949	0.1409	52.9993	7.4700	0.0189
19	7.9108	0.1264	60.0942	7.5964	0.0166
20	8.8206	0.1134	68.0050	7.7098	0.0147
21	9.8349	0.1017	76.8256	7.8115	0.0130
22	10.9660	0.0912	86.6606	7.9027	0.0115
23	12.2271	0.0818	97.6265	7.9845	0.0102
24	13.6332	0.0734	109.8536	8.0578	0.0091
25	15.2010	0.0658	123.4867	8.1236	0.0081
26	16.9491	0.0590	138.6877	8.1826	0.0072
27	18.8982	0.0529	155.6368	8.2355	0.0064
28	21.0715	0.0475	174.5350	8.2830	0.0057
29	23.4948	0.0426	195.6066	8.3255	0.0051
30	26.1967	0.0382	219.1013	8.3637	0.0046
31	29.2093	0.0342	245.2980	8.3979	0.0041
32	32.5683	0.0307	274.5072	8.4287	0.0036
33	36.3137	0.0275	307.0755	8.4562	0.0033
34	40.4898	0.0247	343.3892	8.4809	0.0029
35	45.1461	0.0222	383.8790	8.5030	0.0026
36	50.3379	0.0199	429.0250	8.5229	0.0023
37	56.1267	0.0178	479.3629	8.5407	0.0021
38	62.5813	0.0160	535.4896	8.5567	0.0019
39	69.7782	0.0143	598.0710	8.5710	0.0017
40	77.8027	0.0129	667.8491	8.5839	0.0015
41	86.7500	0.0115	745.6517	8.5954	0.0013
42	96.7262	0.0103	832.4017	8.6058	0.0012
43	107.8497	0.0093	929.1278	8.6150	0.0011
44	120.2524	0.0083	1036.9770	8.6233	0.0010
45	134.0815	0.0075	1157.2300	8.6308	0.0009
46	149.5008	0.0067	1291.3110	8.6375	0.0008
47	166.6934	0.0060	1440.8120	8.6435	0.0007
48	185.8632	0.0054	1607.5050	8.6489	0.0006
49	207.2374	0.0048	1793.3690	8.6537	0.0006
50	231.0697	0.0043	2000.6060	8.6580	0.0005

12%

PERIOD	COMPOUND INTEREST	PRESENT VALUE	AMOUNT OF ANNUITY	PRESENT VALUE OF ANNUITY	SINKING FUND
1	1.1200	0.8929	1.0000	0.8929	1.0000
2	1.2544	0.7972	2.1200	1.6901	0.4717
3	1.4049	0.7118	3.3744	2.4018	0.2963
4	1.5735	0.6355	4.7793	3.0373	0.2092
5	1.7623	0.5674	6.3528	3.6048	0.1574
6	1.9738	0.5066	8.1152	4.1114	0.1232
7	2.2107	0.4523	10.0890	4.5638	0.0991
8	2.4760	0.4039	12.2997	4.9676	0.0813
9	2.7731	0.3606	14.7757	5.3282	0.0677
10	3.1058	0.3220	17.5487	5.6502	0.0570
11	3.4785	0.2875	20.6546	5.9377	0.0484
12	3.8960	0.2567	24.1331	6.1944	0.0414
13	4.3635	0.2292	28.0291	6.4235	0.0357
14	4.8871	0.2046	32.3926	6.6282	0.0309
15	5.4736	0.1827	37.2797	6.8109	0.0268
16	6.1304	0.1631	42.7533	6.9740	0.0234
17	6.8660	0.1456	48.8837	7.1196	0.0205
18	7.6900	0.1300	55.7497	7.2497	0.0179
19	8.6128	0.1161	63.4397	7.3658	0.0158
20	9.6463	0.1037	72.0524	7.4694	0.0139
21	10.8038	0.0926	81.6987	7.5620	0.0122
22	12.1003	0.0826	92.5026	7.6446	0.0108
23	13.5523	0.0738	104.6029	7.7184	0.0096
24	15.1786	0.0659	118.1552	7.7843	0.0085
25	17.0001	0.0588	133.3338	7.8431	0.0075
26	19.0401	0.0525	150.3339	7.8957	0.0067
27	21.3249	0.0469	169.3740	7.9426	0.0059
28	23.8839	0.0419	190.6989	7.9844	0.0052
29	26.7499	0.0374	214.5827	8.0218	0.0047
30	29.9599	0.0334	241.3327	8.0552	0.0041
31	33.5551	0.0298	271.2926	8.0850	0.0037
32	37.5817	0.0266	304.8477	8.1116	0.0033
33	42.0915	0.0238	342.4294	8.1354	0.0029
34	47.1425	0.0212	384.5209	8.1566	0.0026
35	52.7996	0.0189	431.6634	8.1755	0.0023
36	59.1356	0.0169	484.4631	8.1924	0.0021
37	66.2318	0.0151	543.5986	8.2075	0.0018
38	74.1797	0.0135	609.8305	8.2210	0.0016
39	83.0812	0.0120	684.0101	8.2330	0.0015
40	93.0510	0.0107	767.0913	8.2438	0.0013
41	104.2171	0.0096	860.1422	8.2534	0.0012
42	116.7231	0.0086	964.3592	8.2619	0.0010
43	130.7299	0.0076	1081.0820	8.2696	0.0009
44	146.4175	0.0068	1211.8120	8.2764	0.0008
45	163.9876	0.0061	1358.2300	8.2825	0.0007
46	183.6661	0.0054	1522.2170	8.2880	0.0007
47	205.7060	0.0049	1705.8830	8.2928	0.0006
48	230.3908	0.0043	1911.5890	8.2972	0.0005
49	258.0377	0.0039	2141.9800	8.3010	0.0005
50	289.0022	0.0035	2400.0180	8.3045	0.0004

PERIOD	COMPOUND INTEREST	PRESENT VALUE	AMOUNT OF ANNUITY	PRESENT VALUE OF ANNUITY	SINKING FUND
1	1.1250	0.8889	1.0000	0.8889	1.0000
2	1.2656	0.7901	2.1250	1.6790	0.4706
3	1.4238	0.7023	3.3906	2.3813	0.2949
4	1.6018	0.6243	4.8145	3.0056	0.2077
5	1.8020	0.5549	6.4163	3.5606	0.1559
6	2.0273	0.4933	8.2183	4.0538	0.1217
7	2.2807	0.4385	10.2456	4.4923	0.0976
8	2.5658	0.3897	12.5263	4.8820	0.0798
9	2.8865	0.3464	15.0921	5.2285	0.0663
10	3.2473	0.3079	17.9786	5.5364	0.0556
11	3.6532	0.2737	21.2259	5.8102	0.0471
12	4.1099	0.2433	24.8791	6.0535	0.0402
13	4.6236	0.2163	28.9890	6.2698	0.0345
14	5.2016	0.1922	33.6126	6.4620	0.0298
15	5.8518	0.1709	38.8142	6.6329	0.0258
16	6.5833	0.1519	44.6660	6.7848	0.0224
17	7.4062	0.1350	51.2492	6.9198	0.0195
18	8.3319	0.1200	58.6554	7.0398	0.0170
19	9.3734	0.1067	66.9873	7.1465	0.0149
20	10.5451	0.0948	76.3607	7.2414	0.0131
21	11.8632	0.0843	86.9058	7.3256	0.0115
22	13.3461	0.0749	98.7691	7.4006	0.0101
23	15.0144	0.0666	112.1152	7.4672	0.0089
24	16.8912	0.0592	127.1296	7.5264	0.0079
25	19.0026	0.0526	144.0208	7.5790	0.0069
26	21.3779	0.0468	163.0234	7.6258	0.0061
27	24.0502	0.0416	184.4013	7.6674	0.0054
28	27.0564	0.0370	208.4515	7.7043	0.0048
29	30.4385	0.0329	235.5079	7.7372	0.0042
30	34.2433	0.0292	265.9464	7.7664	0.0038
31	38.5237	0.0260	300.1897	7.7923	0.0033
32	43.3392	0.0231	338.7134	7.8154	0.0030
33	48.7566	0.0205	382.0526	7.8359	0.0026
34	54.8512	0.0182	430.8092	7.8542	0.0023
35	61.7075	0.0162	485.6603	7.8704	0.0021
36	69.4210	0.0144	547.3679	7.8848	0.0018
37	78.0986	0.0128	616.7888	7.8976	0.0016
38	87.8609	0.0114	694.8874	7.9089	0.0014
39	98.8436	0.0101	782.7483	7.9191	0.0013
40	111.1990	0.0090	881.5918	7.9281	0.0011
41	125.0989	0.0080	992.7908	7.9360	0.0010
42	140.7362	0.0071	1117.8900	7.9432	0.0009
43	158.3283	0.0063	1258.6260	7.9495	0.0008
44	178.1193	0.0056	1416.9540	7.9551	0.0007
45	200.3842	0.0050	1595.0730	7.9601	0.0006
46	225.4322	0.0044	1795.4580	7.9645	0.0006
47	253.6113	0.0039	2020.8900	7.9685	0.0005
48	285.3127	0.0035	2274.5010	7.9720	0.0004
49	320.9768	0.0031	2559.8140	7.9751	0.0004
50	361.0988	0.0028	2880.7900	7.9778	0.0003

13%

PERIOD	COMPOUND INTEREST	PRESENT VALUE	AMOUNT OF ANNUITY	PRESENT VALUE OF ANNUITY	SINKING FUND
1	1.1300	0.8850	1.0000	0.8850	1.0000
2	1.2769	0.7831	2.1300	1.6681	0.4695
3	1.4429	0.6931	3.4069	2.3612	0.2935
4	1.6305	0.6133	4.8498	2.9745	0.2062
5	1.8424	0.5428	6.4803	3.5172	0.1543
6	2.0820	0.4803	8.3227	3.9975	0.1202
7	2.3526	0.4251	10.4047	4.4226	0.0961
8	2.6584	0.3762	12.7573	4.7988	0.0784
9	3.0040	0.3329	15.4157	5.1317	0.0649
10	3.3946	0.2946	18.4197	5.4262	0.0543
11	3.8359	0.2607	21.8143	5.6869	0.0458
12	4.3345	0.2307	25.6502	5.9176	0.0390
13	4.8980	0.2042	29.9847	6.1218	0.0334
14	5.5348	0.1807	34.8827	6.3025	0.0287
15	6.2543	0.1599	40.4174	6.4624	0.0247
16	7.0673	0.1415	46.6717	6.6039	0.0214
17	7.9861	0.1252	53.7390	6.7291	0.0186
18	9.0243	0.1108	61.7251	6.8399	0.0162
19	10.1974	0.0981	70.7494	6.9380	0.0141
20	11.5231	0.0868	80.9468	7.0248	0.0124
21	13.0211	0.0768	92.4698	7.1015	0.0108
22	14.7138	0.0680	105.4909	7.1695	0.0095
23	16.6266	0.0601	120.2047	7.2297	0.0083
24	18.7881	0.0532	136.8313	7.2829	0.0073
25	21.2305	0.0471	155.6194	7.3300	0.0064
26	23.9905	0.0417	176.8499	7.3717	0.0057
27	27.1093	0.0369	200.8404	7.4086	0.0050
28	30.6335	0.0326	227.9497	7.4412	0.0044
29	34.6158	0.0289	258.5831	7.4701	0.0039
30	39.1159	0.0256	293.1989	7.4957	0.0034
31	44.2009	0.0226	332.3148	7.5183	0.0030
32	49.9470	0.0200	376.5156	7.5383	0.0027
33	56.4402	0.0177	426.4627	7.5560	0.0023
34	63.7774	0.0157	482.9028	7.5717	0.0021
35	72.0684	0.0139	546.6802	7.5856	0.0018
36	81.4373	0.0123	618.7486	7.5979	0.0016
37	92.0242	0.0109	700.1858	7.6087	0.0014
38	103.9873	0.0096	792.2100	7.6183	0.0013
39	117.5057	0.0085	896.1972	7.6268	0.0011
40	132.7814	0.0075	1013.7030	7.6344	0.0010
41	150.0430	0.0067	1146.4840	7.6410	0.0009
42	169.5485	0.0059	1296.5270	7.6469	0.0008
43	191.5899	0.0052	1466.0760	7.6522	0.0007
44	216.4965	0.0046	1657.6650	7.6568	0.0006
45	244.6410	0.0041	1874.1620	7.6609	0.0005
46	276.4444	0.0036	2118.8030	7.6645	0.0005
47	312.3822	0.0032	2395.2470	7.6677	0.0004
48	352.9918	0.0028	2707.6290	7.6705	0.0004
49	398.8807	0.0025	3060.6210	7.6730	0.0003
50	450.7352	0.0022	3459.5010	7.6752	0.0003

PERIOD	COMPOUND INTEREST	PRESENT VALUE	AMOUNT OF ANNUITY	PRESENT VALUE OF ANNUITY	SINKING FUND
1	1.1350	0.8811	1.0000	0.8811	1.0000
2	1.2882	0.7763	2.1350	1.6573	0.4684
3	1.4621	0.6839	3.4232	2.3413	0.2921
4	1.6595	0.6026	4.8854	2.9438	0.2047
5	1.8836	0.5309	6.5449	3.4747	0.1528
6	2.1378	0.4678	8.4284	3.9425	0.1186
7	2.4264	0.4121	10.5663	4.3546	0.0946
8	2.7540	0.3631	12.9927	4.7177	0.0770
9	3.1258	0.3199	15.7467	5.0377	0.0635
10	3.5478	0.2819	18.8726	5.3195	0.0530
11	4.0267	0.2483	22.4204	5.5679	0.0446
12	4.5704	0.2188	26.4471	5.7867	0.0378
13	5.1874	0.1928	31.0175	5.9794	0.0322
14	5.8876	0.1698	36.2048	6.1493	0.0276
15	6.6825	0.1496	42.0925	6.2989	0.0238
16	7.5846	0.1318	48.7749	6.4308	0.0205
17	8.6085	0.1162	56.3596	6.5469	0.0177
18	9.7707	0.1023	64.9681	6.6493	0.0154
19	11.0897	0.0902	74.7388	6.7395	0.0134
20	12.5868	0.0794	85.8285	6.8189	0.0117
21	14.2861	0.0700	98.4154	6.8889	0.0102
22	16.2147	0.0617	112.7014	6.9506	0.0089
23	18.4037	0.0543	128.9161	7.0049	0.0078
24	20.8882	0.0479	147.3198	7.0528	0.0068
25	23.7081	0.0422	168.2080	7.0950	0.0059
26	26.9087	0.0372	191.9160	7.1321	0.0052
27	30.5413	0.0327	218.8247	7.1649	0.0046
28	34.6644	0.0288	249.3660	7.1937	0.0040
29	39.3441	0.0254	284.0304	7.2191	0.0035
30	44.6556	0.0224	323.3745	7.2415	0.0031
31	50.6841	0.0197	368.0301	7.2613	0.0027
32	57.5264	0.0174	418.7141	7.2786	0.0024
33	65.2925	0.0153	476.2405	7.2940	0.0021
34	74.1070	0.0135	541.5330	7.3075	0.0018
35	84.1114	0.0119	615.6400	7.3193	0.0016
36	95.4664	0.0105	699.7513	7.3298	0.0014
37	108.3544	0.0092	795.2177	7.3390	0.0013
38	122.9822	0.0081	903.5720	7.3472	0.0011
39	139.5848	0.0072	1026.5540	7.3543	0.0010
40	158.4288	0.0063	1166.1390	7.3607	0.0009
41	179.8167	0.0056	1324.5680	7.3662	0.0008
42	204.0919	0.0049	1504.3840	7.3711	0.0007
43	231.6443	0.0043	1708.4760	7.3754	0.0006
44	262.9163	0.0038	1940.1210	7.3792	0.0005
45	298.4100	0.0034	2203.0370	7.3826	0.0005
46	338.6953	0.0030	2501.4470	7.3855	0.0004
47	384.4192	0.0026	2840.1420	7.3881	0.0004
48	436.3158	0.0023	3224.5610	7.3904	0.0003
49	495.2184	0.0020	3660.8770	7.3924	0.0003
50	562.0728	0.0018	4156.0950	7.3942	0.0002

14%

PERIOD	COMPOUND INTEREST	PRESENT VALUE	AMOUNT OF ANNUITY	PRESENT VALUE OF ANNUITY	SINKING FUND
1	1.1400	0.8772	1.0000	0.8772	1.0000
2	1.2996	0.7695	2.1400	1.6467	0.4673
3	1.4815	0.6750	3.4396	2.3216	0.2907
4	1.6890	0.5921	4.9211	2.9137	0.2032
5	1.9254	0.5194	6.6101	3.4331	0.1513
6	2.1950	0.4556	8.5355	3.8887	0.1172
7	2.5023	0.3996	10.7305	4.2883	0.0932
8	2.8526	0.3506	13.2328	4.6389	0.0756
9	3.2519	0.3075	16.0853	4.9464	0.0622
10	3.7072	0.2697	19.3373	5.2161	0.0517
11	4.2262	0.2366	23.0445	5.4527	0.0434
12	4.8179	0.2076	27.2708	5.6603	0.0367
13	5.4924	0.1821	32.0887	5.8424	0.0312
14	6.2613	0.1597	37.5811	6.0021	0.0266
15	7.1379	0.1401	43.8424	6.1422	0.0228
16	8.1373	0.1229	50.9804	6.2651	0.0196
17	9.2765	0.1078	59.1176	6.3729	0.0169
18	10.5752	0.0946	68.3941	6.4674	0.0146
19	12.0557	0.0829	78.9692	6.5504	0.0127
20	13.7435	0.0728	91.0249	6.6231	0.0110
21	15.6676	0.0638	104.7684	6.6870	0.0095
22	17.8610	0.0560	120.4360	6.7429	0.0083
23	20.3616	0.0491	138.2971	6.7921	0.0072
24	23.2122	0.0431	158.6587	6.8351	0.0063
25	26.4619	0.0378	181.8708	6.8729	0.0055
26	30.1666	0.0331	208.3328	6.9061	0.0048
27	34.3899	0.0291	238.4994	6.9352	0.0042
28	39.2045	0.0255	272.8893	6.9607	0.0037
29	44.6931	0.0224	312.0938	6.9830	0.0032
30	50.9502	0.0196	356.7869	7.0027	0.0028
31	58.0832	0.0172	407.7371	7.0199	0.0025
32	66.2148	0.0151	465.8203	7.0350	0.0021
33	75.4849	0.0132	532.0351	7.0482	0.0019
34	86.0528	0.0116	607.5200	7.0599	0.0016
35	98.1002	0.0102	693.5728	7.0700	0.0014
36	111.8342	0.0089	791.6730	7.0790	0.0013
37	127.4910	0.0078	903.5072	7.0868	0.0011
38	145.3398	0.0069	1030.9980	7.0937	0.0010
39	165.6873	0.0060	1176.3380	7.0997	0.0009
40	188.8836	0.0053	1342.0250	7.1050	0.0007
41	215.3273	0.0046	1530.9090	7.1097	0.0007
42	245.4731	0.0041	1746.2360	7.1138	0.0006
43	279.8393	0.0036	1991.7090	7.1173	0.0005
44	319.0168	0.0031	2271.5480	7.1205	0.0004
45	363.6792	0.0027	2590.5650	7.1232	0.0004
46	414.5943	0.0024	2954.2450	7.1256	0.0003
47	472.6374	0.0021	3368.8390	7.1277	0.0003
48	538.8066	0.0019	3841.4760	7.1296	0.0003
49	614.2396	0.0016	4380.2830	7.1312	0.0002
50	700.2331	0.0014	4994.5230	7.1327	0.0002

PERIOD	COMPOUND INTEREST	PRESENT VALUE	AMOUNT OF ANNUITY	PRESENT VALUE OF ANNUITY	SINKING FUND
1	1.1450	0.8734	1.0000	0.8734	1.0000
2	1.3110	0.7628	2.1450	1.6361	0.4662
3	1.5011	0.6662	3.4560	2.3023	0.2893
4	1.7188	0.5818	4.9571	2.8841	0.2017
5	1.9680	0.5081	6.6759	3.3922	0.1498
6	2.2534	0.4438	8.6439	3.8360	0.1157
7	2.5801	0.3876	10.8973	4.2236	0.0918
8	2.9542	0.3385	13.4774	4.5621	0.0742
9	3.3826	0.2956	16.4316	4.8577	0.0609
10	3.8731	0.2582	19.8142	5.1159	0.0505
11	4.4347	0.2255	23.6873	5.3414	0.0422
12	5.0777	0.1969	28.1220	5.5383	0.0356
13	5.8139	0.1720	33.1996	5.7103	0.0301
14	6.6570	0.1502	39.0136	5.8606	0.0256
15	7.6222	0.1312	45.6705	5.9918	0.0219
16	8.7275	0.1146	53.2928	6.1063	0.0188
17	9.9929	0.1001	62.0202	6.2064	0.0161
18	11.4419	0.0874	72.0131	6.2938	0.0139
19	13.1010	0.0763	83.4551	6.3701	0.0120
20	15.0006	0.0667	96.5560	6.4368	0.0104
21	17.1757	0.0582	111.5566	6.4950	0.0090
22	19.6662	0.0508	128.7324	6.5459	0.0078
23	22.5178	0.0444	148.3986	6.5903	0.0067
24	25.7829	0.0388	170.9163	6.6291	0.0059
25	29.5214	0.0339	196.6992	6.6629	0.0051
26	33.8020	0.0296	226.2205	6.6925	0.0044
27	38.7033	0.0258	260.0225	6.7184	0.0038
28	44.3152	0.0226	298.7258	6.7409	0.0033
29	50.7409	0.0197	343.0410	6.7606	0.0029
30	58.0984	0.0172	393.7819	6.7778	0.0025
31	66.5226	0.0150	451.8802	6.7929	0.0022
32	76.1684	0.0131	518.4028	6.8060	0.0019
33	87.2128	0.0115	594.5712	6.8175	0.0017
34	99.8587	0.0100	681.7840	6.8275	0.0015
35	114.3382	0.0087	781.6426	6.8362	0.0013
36	130.9172	0.0076	895.9808	6.8439	0.0011
37	149.9002	0.0067	1026.8980	6.8505	0.0010
38	171.6357	0.0058	1176.7980	6.8564	0.0008
39	196.5229	0.0051	1348.4340	6.8615	0.0007
40	225.0187	0.0044	1544.9560	6.8659	0.0006
41	257.6464	0.0039	1769.9750	6.8698	0.0006
42	295.0051	0.0034	2027.6220	6.8732	0.0005
43	337.7808	0.0030	2322.6270	6.8761	0.0004
44	386.7590	0.0026	2660.4070	6.8787	0.0004
45	442.8391	0.0023	3047.1660	6.8810	0.0003
46	507.0507	0.0020	3490.0050	6.8830	0.0003
47	580.5730	0.0017	3997.0550	6.8847	0.0003
48	664.7561	0.0015	4577.6280	6.8862	0.0002
49	761.1456	0.0013	5242.3840	6.8875	0.0002
50	871.5118	0.0011	6003.5300	6.8886	0.0002

15%

PERIOD	COMPOUND INTEREST	PRESENT VALUE	AMOUNT OF ANNUITY	PRESENT VALUE OF ANNUITY	SINKING FUND
1	1.1500	0.8696	1.0000	0.8696	1.0000
2	1.3225	0.7561	2.1500	1.6257	0.4651
3	1.5209	0.6575	3.4725	2.2832	0.2880
4	1.7490	0.5718	4.9934	2.8550	0.2003
5	2.0114	0.4972	6.7424	3.3522	0.1483
6	2.3131	0.4323	8.7537	3.7845	0.1142
7	2.6600	0.3759	11.0668	4.1604	0.0904
8	3.0590	0.3269	13.7268	4.4873	0.0729
9	3.5179	0.2843	16.7858	4.7716	0.0596
10	4.0456	0.2472	20.3037	5.0188	0.0493
11	4.6524	0.2149	24.3493	5.2337	0.0411
12	5.3503	0.1869	29.0017	5.4206	0.0345
13	6.1528	0.1625	34.3519	5.5831	0.0291
14	7.0757	0.1413	40.5047	5.7245	0.0247
15	8.1371	0.1229	47.5804	5.8474	0.0210
16	9.3576	0.1069	55.7175	5.9542	0.0179
17	10.7613	0.0929	65.0751	6.0472	0.0154
18	12.3755	0.0808	75.8364	6.1280	0.0132
19	14.2318	0.0703	88.2118	6.1982	0.0113
20	16.3665	0.0611	102.4436	6.2593	0.0098
21	18.8215	0.0531	118.8101	6.3125	0.0084
22	21.6447	0.0462	137.6317	6.3587	0.0073
23	24.8915	0.0402	159.2764	6.3988	0.0063
24	28.6252	0.0349	184.1679	6.4338	0.0054
25	32.9190	0.0304	212.7930	6.4641	0.0047
26	37.8568	0.0264	245.7120	6.4906	0.0041
27	43.5353	0.0230	283.5688	6.5135	0.0035
28	50.0656	0.0200	327.1041	6.5335	0.0031
29	57.5755	0.0174	377.1697	6.5509	0.0027
30	66.2118	0.0151	434.7452	6.5660	0.0023
31	76.1436	0.0131	500.9570	6.5791	0.0020
32	87.5651	0.0114	577.1005	6.5905	0.0017
33	100.6998	0.0099	664.6656	6.6005	0.0015
34	115.8048	0.0086	765.3654	6.6091	0.0013
35	133.1755	0.0075	881.1702	6.6166	0.0011
36	153.1519	0.0065	1014.3460	6.6231	0.0010
37	176.1246	0.0057	1167.4980	6.6288	0.0009
38	202.5433	0.0049	1343.6220	6.6338	0.0007
39	232.9248	0.0043	1546.1660	6.6380	0.0006
40	267.8636	0.0037	1779.0910	6.6418	0.0006
41	308.0431	0.0032	2046.9540	6.6450	0.0005
42	354.2496	0.0028	2354.9970	6.6478	0.0004
43	407.3870	0.0025	2709.2470	6.6503	0.0004
44	468.4951	0.0021	3116.6340	6.6524	0.0003
45	538.7693	0.0019	3585.1290	6.6543	0.0003
46	619.5847	0.0016	4123.8990	6.6559	0.0002
47	712.5224	0.0014	4743.4830	6.6573	0.0002
48	819.4008	0.0012	5456.0060	6.6585	0.0002
49	942.3109	0.0011	6275.4070	6.6596	0.0002
50	1083.6580	0.0009	7217.7170	6.6605	0.0001

COMMON FRACTION TO DECIMAL CONVERSIONS

Fraction	Decimal equivalent	Fraction	Decimal equivalent	Fraction	Decimal equivalent
$\frac{1}{2}$	.50	$\frac{5}{6}$	$.83\frac{1}{3}(.83\overline{3})$	$\frac{1}{16}$	$.06\frac{1}{4}(.0625)$
$\frac{1}{3}$	$.33\frac{1}{3}(.33\overline{3})$	$\frac{1}{7}$	$.14\frac{2}{7}(.143)$	$\frac{3}{16}$	$.18\frac{3}{4}(.1875)$
$\frac{2}{3}$	$.66\frac{2}{3}(.66\overline{6})$	$\frac{1}{8}$	$.12\frac{1}{2}(.125)$	$\frac{5}{16}$	$.31\frac{1}{4}(.3125)$
$\frac{1}{4}$	.25	$\frac{3}{8}$	$.37\frac{1}{2}(.375)$	$\frac{7}{16}$	$.43\frac{3}{4}(.4375)$
$\frac{3}{4}$	.75	$\frac{5}{8}$	$.62\frac{1}{2}(.625)$	$\frac{9}{16}$	$.56\frac{1}{4}(.5625)$
$\frac{1}{5}$	.20	$\frac{7}{8}$	$.87\frac{1}{2}(.875)$	$\frac{11}{16}$	$.68\frac{3}{4}(.6875)$
$\frac{2}{5}$	.40	$\frac{1}{9}$	$.11\overline{1}$	$\frac{13}{16}$	$.81\frac{1}{4}(.8125)$
$\frac{3}{5}$	.60	$\frac{1}{10}$	.10	$\frac{15}{16}$	$.93\frac{3}{4}(.9375)$
$\frac{4}{5}$	.80	$\frac{1}{12}$	$.08\frac{1}{3}(.08\overline{3})$	$\frac{1}{20}$	.05
$\frac{1}{6}$	$.16\frac{2}{3}(.16\overline{6})$	$\frac{1}{15}$	$.06\frac{2}{3}(.06\overline{6})$	$\frac{1}{25}$	.04

Key Currency Cross Rates   Late New York Trading Wednesday, December 10, 2003

	Dollar	Euro	Pound	SFranc	Peso	Yen	CdnDlr
Canada	1.3075	1.5973	2.2794	1.0316	.11641	.01208	...
Japan	108.27	132.27	188.75	85.427	9.639	...	82.806
Mexico	11.2322	13.7212	19.581	8.8622	...	.10374	8.5904
Switzerland	1.2674	1.5483	2.2095	...	.11284	.01171	.9693
U.K.	.57360	.7007	...	.4526	.05107	.00530	.43871
Euro	.81860	...	1.4271	.64587	.07288	.00756	.62606
U.S.	...	1.2216	1.7433	.78900	.08903	.00924	.76480

Source: Reuters

REFERENCE TABLE OF MEASURES

Measures of length

12 inches = 1 foot	10 millimeters = 1 centimeter
3 feet = 1 yard	10 centimeters = 1 decimeter
1,760 yards = 1 mile	10 decimeters = 1 meter
5,280 feet = 1 mile	1,000 meters = 1 kilometer
	1 inch = 2.54 centimeters

Measures of weight

16 ounces = 1 pound	1,000 milligrams = 1 gram
2,000 pounds = ton	100 centigrams = 1 gram
	1,000 grams = 1 kilogram
	2.2 pounds are about 1 kilogram

Measures of volume (capacity)

8 fluid ounces = 1 cup	1 liter = 1 cubic decimeter
2 cups = 1 pint	1,000 milliliters (cubic centimeters) = 1 liter
2 pints = 1 quart	1,000 liters = 1 kiloliter (cubic meter)
4 quarts = 1 gallon	

Surface measures

144 square inches = 1 square foot	100 square centimeters = 1 square decimeter
9 square feet = 1 square yard	100 square decimeters = 1 square meter
43,560 square feet = 1 acre	
640 acres = 1 square mile	

Time

60 seconds = 1 minute	7 days = 1 week	10 years = 1 decade
60 minutes = 1 hour	365 days = 1 year	100 years = 1 century
24 hours = 1 day	366 days = 1 leap year	1,000 years = 1 millenium

If the wages are—		And the number of withholding allowances claimed is—										
At least	But less than	0	1	2	3	4	5	6	7	8	9	10
		The amount of income tax to be withheld is—										
$600	$610	$78	$67	$58	$50	$41	$32	$23	$14	$8	$2	$0
610	620	80	69	60	51	42	33	24	15	9	3	0
620	630	83	70	61	53	44	35	26	17	10	4	0
630	640	85	72	63	54	45	36	27	18	11	5	0
640	650	88	73	64	56	47	38	29	20	12	6	0
650	660	90	75	66	57	48	39	30	21	13	7	1
660	670	93	78	67	59	50	41	32	23	14	8	2
670	680	95	80	69	60	51	42	33	24	15	9	3
680	690	98	83	70	62	53	44	35	26	17	10	4
690	700	100	85	72	63	54	45	36	27	18	11	5
700	710	103	88	73	65	56	47	38	29	20	12	6
710	720	105	90	75	66	57	48	39	30	21	13	7
720	730	108	93	78	68	59	50	41	32	23	14	8
730	740	110	95	80	69	60	51	42	33	24	15	9
740	750	113	98	83	71	62	53	44	35	26	17	10
750	760	115	100	85	72	63	54	45	36	27	18	11
760	770	118	103	88	74	65	56	47	38	29	20	12
770	780	120	105	90	75	66	57	48	39	30	21	13
780	790	123	108	93	78	68	59	50	41	32	23	14
790	800	125	110	95	80	69	60	51	42	33	24	15
800	810	128	113	98	83	71	62	53	44	35	26	17
810	820	130	115	100	85	72	63	54	45	36	27	18
820	830	133	118	103	88	74	65	56	47	38	29	20
830	840	135	120	105	90	75	66	57	48	39	30	21
840	850	138	123	108	93	78	68	59	50	41	32	23
850	860	140	125	110	95	80	69	60	51	42	33	24
860	870	143	128	113	98	83	71	62	53	44	35	26
870	880	145	130	115	100	85	72	63	54	45	36	27
880	890	148	133	118	103	88	74	65	56	47	38	29
890	900	150	135	120	105	90	76	66	57	48	39	30
900	910	153	138	123	108	93	78	68	59	50	41	32
910	920	155	140	125	110	95	81	69	60	51	42	33
920	930	158	143	128	113	98	83	71	62	53	44	35
930	940	160	145	130	115	100	86	72	63	54	45	36
940	950	163	148	133	118	103	88	74	65	56	47	38
950	960	165	150	135	120	105	91	76	66	57	48	39
960	970	168	153	138	123	108	93	78	68	59	50	41
970	980	170	155	140	125	110	96	81	69	60	51	42
980	990	173	158	143	128	113	98	83	71	62	53	44
990	1,000	175	160	145	130	115	101	86	72	63	54	45
1,000	1,010	178	163	148	133	118	103	88	74	65	56	47
1,010	1,020	180	165	150	135	120	106	91	76	66	57	48
1,020	1,030	183	168	153	138	123	108	93	78	68	59	50
1,030	1,040	185	170	155	140	125	111	96	81	69	60	51
1,040	1,050	188	173	158	143	128	113	98	83	71	62	53
1,050	1,060	190	175	160	145	130	116	101	86	72	63	54
1,060	1,070	193	178	163	148	133	118	103	88	74	65	56
1,070	1,080	195	180	165	150	135	121	106	91	76	66	57
1,080	1,090	198	183	168	153	138	123	108	93	78	68	59
1,090	1,100	200	185	170	155	140	126	111	96	81	69	60
1,100	1,110	203	188	173	158	143	128	113	98	83	71	62
1,110	1,120	205	190	175	160	145	131	116	101	86	72	63
1,120	1,130	208	193	178	163	148	133	118	103	88	74	65
1,130	1,140	210	195	180	165	150	136	121	106	91	76	66
1,140	1,150	213	198	183	168	153	138	123	108	93	78	68
1,150	1,160	215	200	185	170	155	141	126	111	96	81	69
1,160	1,170	218	203	188	173	158	143	128	113	98	83	71
1,170	1,180	220	205	190	175	160	146	131	116	101	86	72
1,180	1,190	223	208	193	178	163	148	133	118	103	88	74
1,190	1,200	225	210	195	180	165	151	136	121	106	91	76
1,200	1,210	228	213	198	183	168	153	138	123	108	93	79
1,210	1,220	230	215	200	185	170	156	141	126	111	96	81
1,220	1,230	233	218	203	188	173	158	143	128	113	98	84
1,230	1,240	235	220	205	190	175	161	146	131	116	101	86
1,240	1,250	238	223	208	193	178	163	148	133	118	103	89

$1,250 and over

32

If the wages are—		And the number of withholding allowances claimed is—										
At least	But less than	0	1	2	3	4	5	6	7	8	9	10
		The amount of income tax to be withheld is—										
$1,420	$1,440	$135	$115	$96	$77	$58	$45	$32	$19	$6	$0	$0
1,440	1,460	138	118	99	80	60	47	34	21	8	0	0
1,460	1,480	141	121	102	83	63	49	36	23	10	0	0
1,480	1,500	144	124	105	86	66	51	38	25	12	0	0
1,500	1,520	147	127	108	89	69	53	40	27	14	1	0
1,520	1,540	150	130	111	92	72	55	42	29	16	3	0
1,540	1,560	153	133	114	95	75	57	44	31	18	5	0
1,560	1,580	156	136	117	98	78	59	46	33	20	7	0
1,580	1,600	159	139	120	101	81	62	48	35	22	9	0
1,600	1,620	162	142	123	104	84	65	50	37	24	11	0
1,620	1,640	165	145	126	107	87	68	52	39	26	13	1
1,640	1,660	168	148	129	110	90	71	54	41	28	15	3
1,660	1,680	171	151	132	113	93	74	56	43	30	17	5
1,680	1,700	174	154	135	116	96	77	58	45	32	19	7
1,700	1,720	177	157	138	119	99	80	60	47	34	21	9
1,720	1,740	180	160	141	122	102	83	63	49	36	23	11
1,740	1,760	183	163	144	125	105	86	66	51	38	25	13
1,760	1,780	186	166	147	128	108	89	69	53	40	27	15
1,780	1,800	189	169	150	131	111	92	72	55	42	29	17
1,800	1,820	192	172	153	134	114	95	75	57	44	31	19
1,820	1,840	195	175	156	137	117	98	78	59	46	33	21
1,840	1,860	198	178	159	140	120	101	81	62	48	35	23
1,860	1,880	201	181	162	143	123	104	84	65	50	37	25
1,880	1,900	204	184	165	146	126	107	87	68	52	39	27
1,900	1,920	207	187	168	149	129	110	90	71	54	41	29
1,920	1,940	210	190	171	152	132	113	93	74	56	43	31
1,940	1,960	213	193	174	155	135	116	96	77	58	45	33
1,960	1,980	216	196	177	158	138	119	99	80	61	47	35
1,980	2,000	219	199	180	161	141	122	102	83	64	49	37
2,000	2,020	222	202	183	164	144	125	105	86	67	51	39
2,020	2,040	225	205	186	167	147	128	108	89	70	53	41
2,040	2,060	228	208	189	170	150	131	111	92	73	55	43
2,060	2,080	231	211	192	173	153	134	114	95	76	57	45
2,080	2,100	234	214	195	176	156	137	117	98	79	59	47
2,100	2,120	237	217	198	179	159	140	120	101	82	62	49
2,120	2,140	240	220	201	182	162	143	123	104	85	65	51
2,140	2,160	243	223	204	185	165	146	126	107	88	68	53
2,160	2,180	246	226	207	188	168	149	129	110	91	71	55
2,180	2,200	249	229	210	191	171	152	132	113	94	74	57
2,200	2,220	252	232	213	194	174	155	135	116	97	77	59
2,220	2,240	255	235	216	197	177	158	138	119	100	80	61
2,240	2,260	258	238	219	200	180	161	141	122	103	83	64
2,260	2,280	261	241	222	203	183	164	144	125	106	86	67
2,280	2,300	264	244	225	206	186	167	147	128	109	89	70
2,300	2,320	267	247	228	209	189	170	150	131	112	92	73
2,320	2,340	270	250	231	212	192	173	153	134	115	95	76
2,340	2,360	273	253	234	215	195	176	156	137	118	98	79
2,360	2,380	276	256	237	218	198	179	159	140	121	101	82
2,380	2,400	279	259	240	221	201	182	162	143	124	104	85
2,400	2,420	282	262	243	224	204	185	165	146	127	107	88
2,420	2,440	285	265	246	227	207	188	168	149	130	110	91
2,440	2,460	288	268	249	230	210	191	171	152	133	113	94
2,460	2,480	291	271	252	233	213	194	174	155	136	116	97
2,480	2,500	294	274	255	236	216	197	177	158	139	119	100
2,500	2,520	297	277	258	239	219	200	180	161	142	122	103
2,520	2,540	300	280	261	242	222	203	183	164	145	125	106
2,540	2,560	303	283	264	245	225	206	186	167	148	128	109
2,560	2,580	306	286	267	248	228	209	189	170	151	131	112
2,580	2,600	309	289	270	251	231	212	192	173	154	134	115
2,600	2,620	312	292	273	254	234	215	195	176	157	137	118
2,620	2,640	315	295	276	257	237	218	198	179	160	140	121
2,640	2,660	318	298	279	260	240	221	201	182	163	143	124
2,660	2,680	321	301	282	263	243	224	204	185	166	146	127
2,680	2,700	324	304	285	266	246	227	207	188	169	149	130
2,700	2,720	328	307	288	269	249	230	210	191	172	152	133
2,720	2,740	333	310	291	272	252	233	213	194	175	155	136

$2,740 and over

PERCENTAGE METHOD INCOME TAX WITHHOLDING TABLE

Payroll Period	One Withholding Allowance
Weekly	$ 59.62
Biweekly	119.23
Semimonthly	129.17
Monthly.	258.33
Quarterly	775.00
Semiannually.	1,500.00
Annually	3,100.00
Daily or miscellaneous (each day of the payroll period)	11.92

TABLE 1—WEEKLY Payroll Period

(a) SINGLE person (including head of household)—

If the amount of wages (after subtracting withholding allowances) is: The amount of income tax to withhold is:

Not over $51 . . . . . $0

Over—	But not over—		of excess over—
$51	—$187 . .	10%	—$51
$187	—$592 . .	$13.60 plus 15%	—$187
$592	—$1,317 . .	$74.35 plus 25%	—$592
$1,317	—$2,860 . .	$255.60 plus 28%	—$1,317
$2,860	—$6,177 . .	$687.64 plus 33%	—$2,860
$6,177	. . . . .	$1,782.25 plus 35%	—$6,177

(b) MARRIED person—

If the amount of wages (after subtracting withholding allowances) is: The amount of income tax to withhold is:

Not over $154 . . . . $0

Over—	But not over—		of excess over—
$154	—$429 . .	10%	—$154
$429	—$1,245 . .	$27.50 plus 15%	—$429
$1,245	—$2,270 . .	$149.90 plus 25%	—$1,245
$2,270	—$3,568 . .	$406.15 plus 28%	—$2,270
$3,568	—$6,271 . .	$769.59 plus 33%	—$3,568
$6,271	. . . . .	$1,661.58 plus 35%	—$6,271

TABLE 2—BIWEEKLY Payroll Period

(a) SINGLE person (including head of household)—

If the amount of wages (after subtracting withholding allowances) is: The amount of income tax to withhold is:

Not over $102 . . . . . $0

Over—	But not over—		of excess over—
$102	—$373 . .	10%	—$102
$373	—$1,185 . .	$27.10 plus 15%	—$373
$1,185	—$2,635 . .	$148.90 plus 25%	—$1,185
$2,635	—$5,719 . .	$511.40 plus 28%	—$2,635
$5,719	—$12,354 . .	$1,374.92 plus 33%	—$5,719
$12,354	. . . . .	$3,564.47 plus 35%	—$12,354

(b) MARRIED person—

If the amount of wages (after subtracting withholding allowances) is: The amount of income tax to withhold is:

Not over $308 . . . . . $0

Over—	But not over—		of excess over—
$308	—$858 . .	10%	—$308
$858	—$2,490 . .	$55.00 plus 15%	—$858
$2,490	—$4,540 . .	$299.80 plus 25%	—$2,490
$4,540	—$7,137 . .	$812.30 plus 28%	—$4,540
$7,137	—$12,542 . .	$1,539.46 plus 33%	—$7,137
$12,542	. . . . .	$3,323.11 plus 35%	—$12,542

TABLE 3—SEMIMONTHLY Payroll Period

(a) SINGLE person (including head of household)—

If the amount of wages (after subtracting withholding allowances) is: The amount of income tax to withhold is:

Not over $110 . . . . . $0

Over—	But not over—		of excess over—
$110	—$404 . .	10%	—$110
$404	—$1,283 . .	$29.40 plus 15%	—$404
$1,283	—$2,854 . .	$161.25 plus 25%	—$1,283
$2,854	—$6,196 . .	$554.00 plus 28%	—$2,854
$6,196	—$13,383 . .	$1,489.76 plus 33%	—$6,196
$13,383	. . . . .	$3,861.47 plus 35%	—$13,383

(b) MARRIED person—

If the amount of wages (after subtracting withholding allowances) is: The amount of income tax to withhold is:

Not over $333 . . . . . $0

Over—	But not over—		of excess over—
$333	—$929 . .	10%	—$333
$929	—$2,698 . .	$59.60 plus 15%	—$929
$2,698	—$4,919 . .	$324.95 plus 25%	—$2,698
$4,919	—$7,731 . .	$880.20 plus 28%	—$4,919
$7,731	—$13,588 . .	$1,667.56 plus 33%	—$7,731
$13,588	. . . . .	$3,600.37 plus 35%	—$13,588

TABLE 4—MONTHLY Payroll Period

(a) SINGLE person (including head of household)—

If the amount of wages (after subtracting withholding allowances) is: The amount of income tax to withhold is:

Not over $221 . . . . . $0'

Over—	But not over—		of excess over—
$221	—$808 . .	10%	—$221
$808	—$2,567 . .	$58.70 plus 15%	—$808
$2,567	—$5,708 . .	$322.55 plus 25%	—$2,567
$5,708	—$12,392 . .	$1,107.80 plus 28%	—$5,708
$12,392	—$26,767 . .	$2,979.32 plus 33%	—$12,392
$26,767	. . . . .	$7,723.07 plus 35%	—$26,767

(b) MARRIED person—

If the amount of wages (after subtracting withholding allowances) is: The amount of income tax to withhold is:

Not over $667 . . . . $0

Over—	But not over—		of excess over—
$667	—$1,858 .	10%	—$667
$1,858	—$5,396 .	$119.10 plus 15%	—$1,858
$5,396	—$9,838 .	$649.80 plus 25%	—$5,396
$9,838	—$15,463 .	$1,760.30 plus 28%	—$9,838
$15,463	—$27,175 .	$3,335.30 plus 33%	—$15,463
$27,175	. . . . .	$7,200.26 plus 35%	—$27,175

INTEREST ON A $1 DEPOSIT COMPOUNDED DAILY—360-DAY BASIS

Number of years	6.00%	6.50%	7.00%	7.50%	8.00%	8.50%	9.00%	9.50%	10.00%
1	1.0618	1.0672	1.0725	1.0779	1.0833	1.0887	1.0942	1.0996	1.1052
2	1.1275	1.1388	1.1503	1.1618	1.1735	1.1853	1.1972	1.2092	1.2214
3	1.1972	1.2153	1.2337	1.2523	1.2712	1.2904	1.3099	1.3297	1.3498
4	1.2712	1.2969	1.3231	1.3498	1.3771	1.4049	1.4333	1.4622	1.4917
5	1.3498	1.3840	1.4190	1.4549	1.4917	1.5295	1.5682	1.6079	1.6486
6	1.4333	1.4769	1.5219	1.5682	1.6160	1.6652	1.7159	1.7681	1.8220
7	1.5219	1.5761	1.6322	1.6904	1.7506	1.8129	1.8775	1.9443	2.0136
8	1.6160	1.6819	1.7506	1.8220	1.8963	1.9737	2.0543	2.1381	2.2253
9	1.7159	1.7949	1.8775	1.9639	2.0543	2.1488	2.2477	2.3511	2.4593
10	1.8220	1.9154	2.0136	2.1168	2.2253	2.3394	2.4593	2.5854	2.7179
15	2.4594	2.6509	2.8574	3.0799	3.3197	3.5782	3.8568	4.1571	4.4808
20	3.3198	3.6689	4.0546	4.4810	4.9522	5.4728	6.0482	6.6842	7.3870
25	4.4811	5.0777	5.7536	6.5195	7.3874	8.3708	9.4851	10.7477	12.1782
30	6.0487	7.0275	8.1645	9.4855	11.0202	12.8032	14.8747	17.2813	20.0772

REBATE FRACTION TABLE BASED ON RULE OF 78

Months to go	Sum of digits	Months to go	Sum of digits	Months to go	Sum of digits	Months to go	Sum of digits
1	1	16	136	31	496	46	1,081
2	3	17	153	32	528	47	1,128
3	6	18	171	33	561	48	1,176
4	10	19	190	34	595	49	1,225
5	15	20	210	35	630	50	1,275
6	21	21	231	36	666	51	1,326
7	28	22	253	37	703	52	1,378
8	36	23	276	38	741	53	1,431
9	45	24	300	39	780	54	1,485
10	55	25	325	40	820	55	1,540
11	66	26	351	41	861	56	1,596
12	78	27	378	42	903	57	1,653
13	91	28	406	43	946	58	1,711
14	105	29	435	44	990	59	1,770
15	120	30	465	45	1,035	60	1,830

THE TAX REFORM ACT UPDATE: ACCELERATED COST RECOVERY SYSTEM FOR ASSETS PLACED IN SERVICE AFTER DECEMBER 31, 1986*

The following classes use a 200% declining-balance, switching to straight-line:

↓

> 3-year: Race horses more than two years old or any horse other than a race horse that is more than 12 years old at time placed into service; special tools of certain industries.
>
> 5-year: Automobiles (not luxury); taxis; light general-purpose trucks, semiconductor manufacturing equipment; computer-based telephone central office switching equipment; qualified technological equipment; property used in connection with research and experimentation.
>
> 7-year: Railroad track; single-purpose agricultural (pigpens) or horticultural structure; fixtures, equipment, and furniture.
>
> 10-year: New law doesn't add any specific property under this class.

The following classes use 150% declining-balance, switching to straight-line:

↓

> 15-year: Municipal wastewater treatment plants; telephone distribution plants and comparable equipment for two-way exchange of voice and data communications.
>
> 20-year: Municipal sewers.

The following classes use straight-line:

↓

> 27.5-year: Only residential rental property.
> 31.5-year: Only nonresidential real property.

*New tax bill of 1989 requires for cellular phones the straight-line depreciation unless 50% is for business use.

MACRS

Year of recovery	3-year	5-year	7-year	10-year	15-year	20-year
1	33%	20.00%	14.28%	10.00%	5.00%	3.75%
2	45%	32.00%	24.49%	18.00%	9.50%	7.22%
3	15%	19.20%	17.49%	14.40%	8.55%	6.68%
4	7%	11.52%	12.49%	11.52%	7.69%	6.18%
5		11.52%	8.93%	9.22%	6.93%	5.71%
6		5.76%	8.93%	7.37%	6.23%	5.28%
7			8.93%	6.55%	5.90%	4.89%
8			4.46%	6.55%	5.90%	4.52%
9				6.55%	5.90%	4.46%
10				6.55%	5.90%	4.46%
11				3.29%	5.90%	4.46%
12					5.90%	4.46%
13					5.90%	4.46%
14					5.90%	4.46%
15					5.90%	4.46%
16					3.00%	4.46%
17						4.46%
18						4.46%
19						4.46%
20						4.46%
21						2.25%

NUMBER OF PAYMENTS	ANNUAL PERCENTAGE RATE															
	2.00%	2.25%	2.50%	2.75%	3.00%	3.25%	3.50%	3.75%	4.00%	4.25%	4.50%	4.75%	5.00%	5.25%	5.50%	5.75%
	(FINANCE CHARGE PER $100 OF AMOUNT FINANCED)															
1	0.17	0.19	0.21	0.23	0.25	0.27	0.29	0.31	0.33	0.35	0.37	0.40	0.42	0.44	0.46	0.48
2	0.25	0.28	0.31	0.34	0.38	0.41	0.44	0.47	0.50	0.53	0.56	0.59	0.63	0.66	0.69	0.72
3	0.33	0.38	0.42	0.46	0.50	0.54	0.58	0.63	0.67	0.71	0.75	0.79	0.83	0.88	0.92	0.96
4	0.42	0.47	0.52	0.57	0.63	0.68	0.73	0.78	0.83	0.89	0.94	0.99	1.04	1.10	1.15	1.20
5	0.50	0.56	0.63	0.69	0.75	0.81	0.88	0.94	1.00	1.07	1.13	1.19	1.25	1.32	1.39	1.44
6	0.58	0.66	0.73	0.80	0.88	0.95	1.02	1.10	1.17	1.24	1.32	1.39	1.46	1.54	1.61	1.68
7	0.67	0.75	0.84	0.92	1.00	1.09	1.17	1.25	1.34	1.42	1.51	1.59	1.67	1.76	1.84	1.93
8	0.75	0.85	0.94	1.03	1.13	1.22	1.32	1.41	1.51	1.60	1.69	1.79	1.88	1.98	2.07	2.17
9	0.84	0.94	1.04	1.15	1.25	1.36	1.46	1.57	1.67	1.78	1.88	1.99	2.09	2.20	2.31	2.41
10	0.92	1.03	1.15	1.26	1.38	1.50	1.61	1.73	1.84	1.96	2.07	2.19	2.31	2.42	2.54	2.65
11	1.00	1.13	1.25	1.38	1.51	1.63	1.76	1.88	2.01	2.14	2.26	2.39	2.52	2.64	2.77	2.90
12	1.09	1.22	1.36	1.50	1.63	1.77	1.91	2.04	2.18	2.32	2.45	2.59	2.73	2.87	3.00	3.14
13	1.17	1.32	1.46	1.61	1.76	1.91	2.05	2.20	2.35	2.50	2.64	2.79	2.94	3.09	3.24	3.39
14	1.25	1.41	1.57	1.73	1.89	2.04	2.20	2.36	2.52	2.68	2.84	2.99	3.15	3.31	3.47	3.63
15	1.34	1.51	1.67	1.84	2.01	2.18	2.35	2.52	2.69	2.86	3.03	3.20	3.37	3.54	3.71	3.88
16	1.42	1.60	1.78	1.96	2.14	2.32	2.50	2.68	2.86	3.04	3.22	3.40	3.58	3.76	3.94	4.12
17	1.51	1.70	1.89	2.08	2.26	2.46	2.65	2.84	3.03	3.22	3.41	3.60	3.79	3.98	4.18	4.37
18	1.59	1.79	1.99	2.19	2.39	2.59	2.79	2.99	3.20	3.40	3.60	3.80	4.00	4.21	4.41	4.61
19	1.67	1.89	2.10	2.31	2.52	2.73	2.94	3.15	3.37	3.58	3.79	4.01	4.22	4.43	4.65	4.86
20	1.76	1.98	2.20	2.42	2.65	2.87	3.09	3.31	3.54	3.76	3.98	4.21	4.43	4.66	4.88	5.11
21	1.84	2.08	2.31	2.54	2.77	3.01	3.24	3.47	3.71	3.94	4.18	4.41	4.65	4.88	5.12	5.35
22	1.93	2.17	2.41	2.66	2.90	3.14	3.39	3.63	3.88	4.12	4.37	4.62	4.86	5.11	5.36	5.60
23	2.01	2.27	2.52	2.77	3.03	3.28	3.54	3.79	4.05	4.31	4.56	4.82	5.08	5.33	5.59	5.85
24	2.10	2.36	2.62	2.89	3.15	3.42	3.69	3.95	4.22	4.49	4.75	5.02	5.29	5.56	5.83	6.10
25	2.18	2.46	2.73	3.01	3.28	3.56	3.84	4.11	4.39	4.67	4.95	5.23	5.51	5.79	6.07	6.35
26	2.27	2.55	2.84	3.12	3.41	3.70	3.99	4.27	4.56	4.85	5.14	5.43	5.72	6.01	6.31	6.60
27	2.35	2.65	2.94	3.24	3.54	3.84	4.13	4.43	4.73	5.03	5.34	5.64	5.94	6.24	6.54	6.85
28	2.43	2.74	3.05	3.36	3.67	3.97	4.28	4.59	4.91	5.22	5.53	5.84	6.15	6.47	6.78	7.10
29	2.52	2.84	3.16	3.47	3.79	4.11	4.43	4.76	5.08	5.40	5.72	6.05	6.37	6.70	7.02	7.35
30	2.60	2.93	3.26	3.59	3.92	4.25	4.58	4.92	5.25	5.58	5.92	6.25	6.59	6.92	7.26	7.60
31	2.69	3.03	3.37	3.71	4.05	4.39	4.73	5.08	5.42	5.77	6.11	6.46	6.81	7.15	7.50	7.85
32	2.77	3.12	3.47	3.83	4.18	4.53	4.88	5.24	5.59	5.95	6.31	6.66	7.02	7.38	7.74	8.10
33	2.86	3.22	3.58	3.94	4.31	4.67	5.04	5.40	5.77	6.13	6.50	6.87	7.24	7.61	7.98	8.35
34	2.94	3.32	3.69	4.06	4.44	4.81	5.19	5.56	5.94	6.32	6.70	7.08	7.46	7.84	8.22	8.61
35	3.03	3.41	3.79	4.18	4.56	4.95	5.34	5.72	6.11	6.50	6.89	7.28	7.68	8.07	8.46	8.86
36	3.11	3.51	3.90	4.30	4.69	5.09	5.49	5.89	6.29	6.69	7.09	7.49	7.90	8.30	8.71	9.11
37	3.20	3.60	4.01	4.41	4.82	5.23	5.64	6.05	6.46	6.87	7.28	7.70	8.11	8.53	8.95	9.37
38	3.28	3.70	4.11	4.53	4.95	5.37	5.79	6.21	6.63	7.06	7.48	7.91	8.33	8.76	9.19	9.62
39	3.37	3.79	4.22	4.65	5.08	5.51	5.94	6.37	6.81	7.24	7.68	8.11	8.55	8.99	9.43	9.87
40	3.45	3.89	4.33	4.77	5.21	5.65	6.09	6.54	6.98	7.43	7.87	8.32	8.77	9.22	9.67	10.13
41	3.54	3.99	4.44	4.89	5.34	5.79	6.24	6.70	7.16	7.61	8.07	8.53	8.99	9.45	9.92	10.38
42	3.62	4.08	4.54	5.00	5.47	5.93	6.40	6.86	7.33	7.80	8.27	8.74	9.21	9.69	10.16	10.64
43	3.71	4.18	4.65	5.12	5.60	6.07	6.55	7.03	7.50	7.98	8.47	8.95	9.43	9.92	10.41	10.89
44	3.79	4.28	4.76	5.24	5.73	6.21	6.70	7.19	7.68	8.17	8.66	9.16	9.65	10.15	10.65	11.15
45	3.88	4.37	4.86	5.36	5.86	6.35	6.85	7.35	7.85	8.36	8.86	9.37	9.88	10.38	10.89	11.41
46	3.97	4.47	4.97	5.48	5.98	6.49	7.00	7.52	8.03	8.54	9.06	9.58	10.10	10.62	11.14	11.66
47	4.05	4.56	5.08	5.60	6.11	6.63	7.16	7.68	8.20	8.73	9.26	9.79	10.32	10.85	11.39	11.92
48	4.14	4.66	5.19	5.72	6.24	6.78	7.31	7.84	8.38	8.92	9.46	10.00	10.54	11.09	11.63	12.18
49	4.22	4.76	5.30	5.83	6.37	6.92	7.46	8.01	8.56	9.10	9.66	10.21	10.76	11.32	11.88	12.44
50	4.31	4.85	5.40	5.95	6.50	7.06	7.61	8.17	8.73	9.29	9.85	10.42	10.99	11.55	12.12	12.70
51	4.39	4.95	5.51	6.07	6.64	7.20	7.77	8.34	8.91	9.48	10.05	10.63	11.21	11.79	12.37	12.95
52	4.48	5.05	5.62	6.19	6.77	7.34	7.92	8.50	9.08	9.67	10.25	10.84	11.43	12.02	12.62	13.21
53	4.56	5.14	5.73	6.31	6.90	7.48	8.07	8.67	9.26	9.86	10.45	11.05	11.66	12.26	12.86	13.47
54	4.65	5.24	5.83	6.43	7.03	7.63	8.23	8.83	9.44	10.04	10.65	11.26	11.88	12.49	13.11	13.73
55	4.74	5.34	5.94	6.55	7.16	7.77	8.38	9.00	9.61	10.23	10.85	11.48	12.10	12.73	13.36	13.99
56	4.82	5.44	6.05	6.67	7.29	7.91	8.53	9.16	9.79	10.42	11.05	11.69	12.33	12.97	13.61	14.25
57	4.91	5.53	6.16	6.79	7.42	8.05	8.69	9.33	9.97	10.61	11.25	11.90	12.55	13.20	13.86	14.52
58	4.99	5.63	6.27	6.91	7.55	8.19	8.84	9.49	10.14	10.80	11.46	12.11	12.78	13.44	14.11	14.78
59	5.08	5.73	6.38	7.03	7.68	8.34	9.00	9.66	10.32	10.99	11.66	12.33	13.00	13.68	14.36	15.04
60	5.17	5.82	6.48	7.15	7.81	8.48	9.15	9.82	10.50	11.18	11.86	12.54	13.23	13.92	14.61	15.30

NUMBER OF PAYMENTS	ANNUAL PERCENTAGE RATE															
	6.00%	6.25%	6.50%	6.75%	7.00%	7.25%	7.50%	7.75%	8.00%	8.25%	8.50%	8.75%	9.00%	9.25%	9.50%	9.75%
	(FINANCE CHARGE PER $100 OF AMOUNT FINANCED)															
1	0.50	0.52	0.54	0.56	0.58	0.60	0.62	0.65	0.67	0.69	0.71	0.73	0.75	0.77	0.79	0.81
2	0.75	0.78	0.81	0.84	0.88	0.91	0.94	0.97	1.00	1.03	1.06	1.10	1.13	1.16	1.19	1.22
3	1.00	1.04	1.09	1.13	1.17	1.21	1.25	1.29	1.34	1.38	1.42	1.46	1.50	1.55	1.59	1.63
4	1.25	1.31	1.36	1.41	1.46	1.51	1.57	1.62	1.67	1.72	1.78	1.83	1.88	1.93	1.99	2.04
5	1.50	1.57	1.63	1.69	1.76	1.82	1.88	1.95	2.01	2.07	2.13	2.20	2.26	2.32	2.39	2.45
6	1.76	1.83	1.90	1.98	2.05	2.13	2.20	2.27	2.35	2.42	2.49	2.57	2.64	2.72	2.79	2.86
7	2.01	2.09	2.18	2.26	2.35	2.43	2.52	2.60	2.68	2.77	2.85	2.94	3.02	3.11	3.19	3.28
8	2.26	2.36	2.45	2.55	2.64	2.74	2.83	2.93	3.02	3.12	3.21	3.31	3.40	3.50	3.60	3.69
9	2.52	2.62	2.73	2.83	2.94	3.05	3.15	3.26	3.36	3.47	3.57	3.68	3.79	3.89	4.00	4.11
10	2.77	2.89	3.00	3.12	3.24	3.35	3.47	3.59	3.70	3.82	3.94	4.05	4.17	4.29	4.41	4.52
11	3.02	3.15	3.28	3.41	3.53	3.66	3.79	3.92	4.04	4.17	4.30	4.43	4.56	4.68	4.81	4.94
12	3.28	3.42	3.56	3.69	3.83	3.97	4.11	4.25	4.39	4.52	4.66	4.80	4.94	5.08	5.22	5.36
13	3.53	3.68	3.83	3.98	4.13	4.28	4.43	4.58	4.73	4.88	5.03	5.18	5.33	5.48	5.63	5.78
14	3.79	3.95	4.11	4.27	4.43	4.59	4.75	4.91	5.07	5.23	5.39	5.55	5.72	5.88	6.04	6.20
15	4.05	4.22	4.39	4.56	4.73	4.90	5.07	5.24	5.42	5.59	5.76	5.93	6.10	6.28	6.45	6.62
16	4.30	4.48	4.67	4.85	5.03	5.21	5.40	5.58	5.76	5.94	6.13	6.31	6.49	6.68	6.86	7.05
17	4.56	4.75	4.95	5.14	5.33	5.52	5.72	5.91	6.11	6.30	6.49	6.69	6.88	7.08	7.27	7.47
18	4.82	5.02	5.22	5.43	5.63	5.84	6.04	6.25	6.45	6.66	6.86	7.07	7.28	7.48	7.69	7.90
19	5.07	5.29	5.50	5.72	5.94	6.15	6.37	6.58	6.80	7.02	7.23	7.45	7.67	7.89	8.10	8.32
20	5.33	5.56	5.78	6.01	6.24	6.46	6.69	6.92	7.15	7.38	7.60	7.83	8.06	8.29	8.52	8.75
21	5.59	5.83	6.07	6.30	6.54	6.78	7.02	7.26	7.50	7.74	7.97	8.21	8.46	8.70	8.94	9.18
22	5.85	6.10	6.35	6.60	6.84	7.09	7.34	7.59	7.84	8.10	8.35	8.60	8.85	9.10	9.36	9.61
23	6.11	6.37	6.63	6.89	7.15	7.41	7.67	7.93	8.19	8.46	8.72	8.98	9.25	9.51	9.77	10.04
24	6.37	6.64	6.91	7.18	7.45	7.73	8.00	8.27	8.55	8.82	9.09	9.37	9.64	9.92	10.19	10.47
25	6.63	6.91	7.19	7.48	7.76	8.04	8.33	8.61	8.90	9.18	9.47	9.75	10.04	10.33	10.62	10.90
26	6.89	7.18	7.48	7.77	8.07	8.36	8.66	8.95	9.25	9.55	9.84	10.14	10.44	10.74	11.04	11.34
27	7.15	7.46	7.76	8.07	8.37	8.68	8.99	9.29	9.60	9.91	10.22	10.53	10.84	11.15	11.46	11.77
28	7.41	7.73	8.05	8.36	8.68	9.00	9.32	9.64	9.96	10.28	10.60	10.92	11.24	11.56	11.89	12.21
29	7.67	8.00	8.33	8.66	8.99	9.32	9.65	9.98	10.31	10.64	10.97	11.31	11.64	11.98	12.31	12.65
30	7.94	8.28	8.61	8.96	9.30	9.64	9.98	10.32	10.66	11.01	11.35	11.70	12.04	12.39	12.74	13.09
31	8.20	8.55	8.90	9.25	9.60	9.96	10.31	10.67	11.02	11.38	11.73	12.09	12.45	12.81	13.17	13.53
32	8.46	8.82	9.19	9.55	9.91	10.28	10.64	11.01	11.38	11.74	12.11	12.48	12.85	13.22	13.59	13.97
33	8.73	9.10	9.47	9.85	10.22	10.60	10.98	11.36	11.73	12.11	12.49	12.88	13.26	13.64	14.02	14.41
34	8.99	9.37	9.76	10.15	10.53	10.92	11.31	11.70	12.09	12.48	12.88	13.27	13.66	14.06	14.45	14.85
35	9.25	9.65	10.05	10.45	10.85	11.25	11.65	12.05	12.45	12.85	13.26	13.66	14.07	14.48	14.89	15.29
36	9.52	9.93	10.34	10.75	11.16	11.57	11.98	12.40	12.81	13.23	13.64	14.06	14.48	14.90	15.32	15.74
37	9.78	10.20	10.63	11.05	11.47	11.89	12.32	12.74	13.17	13.60	14.03	14.46	14.89	15.32	15.75	16.19
38	10.05	10.48	10.91	11.35	11.78	12.22	12.66	13.09	13.53	13.97	14.41	14.85	15.30	15.74	16.19	16.63
39	10.32	10.76	11.20	11.65	12.10	12.54	12.99	13.44	13.89	14.35	14.80	15.25	15.71	16.17	16.62	17.08
40	10.58	11.04	11.49	11.95	12.41	12.87	13.33	13.79	14.26	14.72	15.19	15.65	16.12	16.59	17.06	17.53
41	10.85	11.32	11.78	12.25	12.72	13.20	13.67	14.14	14.62	15.10	15.57	16.05	16.53	17.01	17.50	17.98
42	11.12	11.60	12.08	12.56	13.04	13.52	14.01	14.50	14.98	15.47	15.96	16.45	16.95	17.44	17.94	18.43
43	11.38	11.87	12.37	12.86	13.36	13.85	14.35	14.85	15.35	15.85	16.35	16.86	17.36	17.87	18.38	18.89
44	11.65	12.15	12.66	13.16	13.67	14.18	14.69	15.20	15.71	16.23	16.74	17.26	17.78	18.30	18.82	19.34
45	11.92	12.44	12.95	13.47	13.99	14.51	15.03	15.55	16.08	16.61	17.13	17.66	18.19	18.73	19.26	19.79
46	12.19	12.72	13.24	13.77	14.31	14.84	15.37	15.91	16.45	16.99	17.53	18.07	18.61	19.16	19.70	20.25
47	12.46	13.00	13.54	14.08	14.62	15.17	15.72	16.26	16.81	17.37	17.92	18.47	19.03	19.59	20.15	20.71
48	12.73	13.28	13.83	14.39	14.94	15.50	16.06	16.62	17.18	17.75	18.31	18.88	19.45	20.02	20.59	21.16
49	13.00	13.56	14.13	14.69	15.26	15.83	16.40	16.98	17.55	18.13	18.71	19.29	19.87	20.45	21.04	21.62
50	13.27	13.84	14.42	15.00	15.58	16.16	16.75	17.33	17.92	18.51	19.10	19.69	20.29	20.89	21.48	22.08
51	13.54	14.13	14.72	15.31	15.90	16.50	17.09	17.69	18.29	18.89	19.50	20.10	20.71	21.32	21.93	22.55
52	13.81	14.41	15.01	15.62	16.22	16.83	17.44	18.05	18.66	19.28	19.89	20.51	21.13	21.76	22.38	23.01
53	14.08	14.69	15.31	15.92	16.54	17.16	17.78	18.41	19.03	19.66	20.29	20.92	21.56	22.19	22.83	23.47
54	14.36	14.98	15.61	16.23	16.86	17.50	18.13	18.77	19.41	20.05	20.69	21.34	21.98	22.63	23.28	23.94
55	14.63	15.26	15.90	16.54	17.19	17.83	18.48	19.13	19.78	20.43	21.09	21.75	22.41	23.07	23.73	24.40
56	14.90	15.55	16.20	16.85	17.51	18.17	18.83	19.49	20.15	20.82	21.49	22.16	22.83	23.51	24.19	24.87
57	15.17	15.84	16.50	17.17	17.83	18.50	19.18	19.85	20.53	21.21	21.89	22.58	23.26	23.95	24.64	25.34
58	15.45	16.12	16.80	17.48	18.16	18.84	19.53	20.21	20.91	21.60	22.29	22.99	23.69	24.39	25.10	25.80
59	15.72	16.41	17.10	17.79	18.48	19.18	19.88	20.58	21.28	21.99	22.70	23.41	24.12	24.84	25.55	26.27
60	16.00	16.70	17.40	18.10	18.81	19.52	20.23	20.94	21.66	22.38	23.10	23.82	24.55	25.28	26.01	26.75

NUMBER OF PAYMENTS	10.00%	10.25%	10.50%	10.75%	11.00%	11.25%	11.50%	11.75%	12.00%	12.25%	12.50%	12.75%	13.00%	13.25%	13.50%	13.75%
	(FINANCE CHARGE PER $100 OF AMOUNT FINANCED)															
1	0.83	0.85	0.87	0.90	0.92	0.94	0.96	0.98	1.00	1.02	1.04	1.06	1.08	1.10	1.12	1.15
2	1.25	1.28	1.31	1.35	1.38	1.41	1.44	1.47	1.50	1.53	1.57	1.60	1.63	1.66	1.69	1.72
3	1.67	1.71	1.76	1.80	1.84	1.88	1.92	1.96	2.01	2.05	2.09	2.13	2.17	2.22	2.26	2.30
4	2.09	2.14	2.20	2.25	2.30	2.35	2.41	2.46	2.51	2.57	2.62	2.67	2.72	2.78	2.83	2.88
5	2.51	2.58	2.64	2.70	2.77	2.83	2.89	2.96	3.02	3.08	3.15	3.21	3.27	3.34	3.40	3.46
6	2.94	3.01	3.08	3.16	3.23	3.31	3.38	3.45	3.53	3.60	3.68	3.75	3.83	3.90	3.97	4.05
7	3.36	3.45	3.53	3.62	3.70	3.78	3.87	3.95	4.04	4.12	4.21	4.29	4.38	4.47	4.55	4.64
8	3.79	3.88	3.98	4.07	4.17	4.26	4.36	4.46	4.55	4.65	4.74	4.84	4.94	5.03	5.13	5.22
9	4.21	4.32	4.43	4.53	4.64	4.75	4.85	4.96	5.07	5.17	5.28	5.39	5.49	5.60	5.71	5.82
10	4.64	4.76	4.88	4.99	5.11	5.23	5.35	5.46	5.58	5.70	5.82	5.94	6.05	6.17	6.29	6.41
11	5.07	5.20	5.33	5.45	5.58	5.71	5.84	5.97	6.10	6.23	6.36	6.49	6.62	6.75	6.88	7.01
12	5.50	5.64	5.78	5.92	6.06	6.20	6.34	6.48	6.62	6.76	6.90	7.04	7.18	7.32	7.46	7.60
13	5.93	6.08	6.23	6.38	6.53	6.68	6.84	6.99	7.14	7.29	7.44	7.59	7.75	7.90	8.05	8.20
14	6.36	6.52	6.69	6.85	7.01	7.17	7.34	7.50	7.66	7.82	7.99	8.15	8.31	8.48	8.64	8.81
15	6.80	6.97	7.14	7.32	7.49	7.66	7.84	8.01	8.19	8.36	8.53	8.71	8.88	9.06	9.23	9.41
16	7.23	7.41	7.60	7.78	7.97	8.15	8.34	8.53	8.71	8.90	9.08	9.27	9.46	9.64	9.83	10.02
17	7.67	7.86	8.06	8.25	8.45	8.65	8.84	9.04	9.24	9.44	9.63	9.83	10.03	10.23	10.43	10.63
18	8.10	8.31	8.52	8.73	8.93	9.14	9.35	9.56	9.77	9.98	10.19	10.40	10.61	10.82	11.03	11.24
19	8.54	8.76	8.98	9.20	9.42	9.64	9.86	10.08	10.30	10.52	10.74	10.96	11.18	11.41	11.63	11.85
20	8.98	9.21	9.44	9.67	9.90	10.13	10.37	10.60	10.83	11.06	11.30	11.53	11.76	12.00	12.23	12.46
21	9.42	9.66	9.90	10.15	10.39	10.63	10.88	11.12	11.36	11.61	11.85	12.10	12.34	12.59	12.84	13.08
22	9.86	10.12	10.37	10.62	10.88	11.13	11.39	11.64	11.90	12.16	12.41	12.67	12.93	13.19	13.44	13.70
23	10.30	10.57	10.84	11.10	11.37	11.63	11.90	12.17	12.44	12.71	12.97	13.24	13.51	13.78	14.05	14.32
24	10.75	11.02	11.30	11.58	11.86	12.14	12.42	12.70	12.98	13.26	13.54	13.82	14.10	14.38	14.66	14.95
25	11.19	11.48	11.77	12.06	12.35	12.64	12.93	13.22	13.52	13.81	14.10	14.40	14.69	14.98	15.28	15.57
26	11.64	11.94	12.24	12.54	12.85	13.15	13.45	13.75	14.06	14.36	14.67	14.97	15.28	15.59	15.89	16.20
27	12.09	12.40	12.71	13.03	13.34	13.66	13.97	14.29	14.60	14.92	15.24	15.56	15.87	16.19	16.51	16.83
28	12.53	12.86	13.18	13.51	13.84	14.16	14.49	14.82	15.15	15.48	15.81	16.14	16.47	16.80	17.13	17.46
29	12.98	13.32	13.66	14.00	14.33	14.67	15.01	15.35	15.70	16.04	16.38	16.72	17.07	17.41	17.75	18.10
30	13.43	13.78	14.13	14.48	14.83	15.19	15.54	15.89	16.24	16.60	16.95	17.31	17.66	18.02	18.38	18.74
31	13.89	14.25	14.61	14.97	15.33	15.70	16.06	16.43	16.79	17.16	17.53	17.90	18.27	18.63	19.00	19.38
32	14.34	14.71	15.09	15.46	15.84	16.21	16.59	16.97	17.35	17.73	18.11	18.49	18.87	19.25	19.63	20.02
33	14.79	15.18	15.57	15.95	16.34	16.73	17.12	17.51	17.90	18.29	18.69	19.08	19.47	19.87	20.26	20.66
34	15.25	15.65	16.05	16.44	16.85	17.25	17.65	18.05	18.46	18.86	19.27	19.67	20.08	20.49	20.90	21.31
35	15.70	16.11	16.53	16.94	17.35	17.77	18.18	18.60	19.01	19.43	19.85	20.27	20.69	21.11	21.53	21.95
36	16.16	16.58	17.01	17.43	17.86	18.29	18.71	19.14	19.57	20.00	20.43	20.87	21.30	21.73	22.17	22.60
37	16.62	17.06	17.49	17.93	18.37	18.81	19.25	19.69	20.13	20.58	21.02	21.46	21.91	22.36	22.81	23.25
38	17.08	17.53	17.98	18.43	18.88	19.33	19.78	20.24	20.69	21.15	21.61	22.07	22.52	22.99	23.45	23.91
39	17.54	18.00	18.46	18.93	19.39	19.86	20.32	20.79	21.26	21.73	22.20	22.67	23.14	23.61	24.09	24.56
40	18.00	18.48	18.95	19.43	19.90	20.38	20.86	21.34	21.82	22.30	22.79	23.27	23.76	24.24	24.73	25.22
41	18.47	18.95	19.44	19.93	20.42	20.91	21.40	21.89	22.39	22.88	23.38	23.88	24.38	24.88	25.38	25.88
42	18.93	19.43	19.93	20.43	20.93	21.44	21.94	22.45	22.96	23.47	23.98	24.49	25.00	25.51	26.03	26.55
43	19.40	19.91	20.42	20.94	21.45	21.97	22.49	23.01	23.53	24.05	24.57	25.10	25.62	26.15	26.68	27.21
44	19.86	20.39	20.91	21.44	21.97	22.50	23.03	23.57	24.10	24.64	25.17	25.71	26.25	26.79	27.33	27.88
45	20.33	20.87	21.41	21.95	22.49	23.03	23.58	24.12	24.67	25.22	25.77	26.32	26.88	27.43	27.99	28.55
46	20.80	21.35	21.90	22.46	23.01	23.57	24.13	24.69	25.25	25.81	26.37	26.94	27.51	28.08	28.65	29.22
47	21.27	21.83	22.40	22.97	23.53	24.10	24.68	25.25	25.82	26.40	26.98	27.56	28.14	28.72	29.31	29.89
48	21.74	22.32	22.90	23.48	24.06	24.64	25.23	25.81	26.40	26.99	27.58	28.18	28.77	29.37	29.97	30.57
49	22.21	22.80	23.39	23.99	24.58	25.18	25.78	26.38	26.98	27.59	28.19	28.80	29.41	30.02	30.63	31.24
50	22.69	23.29	23.89	24.50	25.11	25.72	26.33	26.95	27.56	28.18	28.80	29.42	30.04	30.67	31.29	31.92
51	23.16	23.78	24.40	25.02	25.64	26.26	26.89	27.52	28.15	28.78	29.41	30.05	30.68	31.32	31.96	32.60
52	23.64	24.27	24.90	25.53	26.17	26.81	27.45	28.09	28.73	29.38	30.02	30.67	31.32	31.98	32.63	33.29
53	24.11	24.76	25.40	26.05	26.70	27.35	28.00	28.66	29.32	29.98	30.64	31.30	31.97	32.63	33.30	33.97
54	24.59	25.25	25.91	26.57	27.23	27.90	28.56	29.23	29.91	30.58	31.25	31.93	32.61	33.29	33.98	34.66
55	25.07	25.74	26.41	27.09	27.77	28.44	29.13	29.81	30.50	31.18	31.87	32.56	33.26	33.95	34.65	35.35
56	25.55	26.23	26.92	27.61	28.30	28.99	29.69	30.39	31.09	31.79	32.49	33.20	33.91	34.62	35.33	36.04
57	26.03	26.73	27.43	28.13	28.84	29.54	30.25	30.97	31.68	32.39	33.11	33.83	34.56	35.28	36.01	36.74
58	26.51	27.23	27.94	28.66	29.37	30.10	30.82	31.55	32.27	33.00	33.74	34.47	35.21	35.95	36.69	37.43
59	27.00	27.72	28.45	29.18	29.91	30.65	31.39	32.13	32.87	33.61	34.36	35.11	35.86	36.62	37.37	38.13
60	27.48	28.22	28.96	29.71	30.45	31.20	31.96	32.71	33.47	34.23	34.99	35.75	36.52	37.29	38.06	38.83

NUMBER OF PAYMENTS	ANNUAL PERCENTAGE RATE															
	14.00%	14.25%	14.50%	14.75%	15.00%	15.25%	15.50%	15.75%	16.00%	16.25%	16.50%	16.75%	17.00%	17.25%	17.50%	17.75%
	(FINANCE CHARGE PER $100 OF AMOUNT FINANCED)															
1	1.17	1.19	1.21	1.23	1.25	1.27	1.29	1.31	1.33	1.35	1.37	1.40	1.42	1.44	1.46	1.48
2	1.75	1.78	1.82	1.85	1.88	1.91	1.94	1.97	2.00	2.04	2.07	2.10	2.13	2.16	2.19	2.22
3	2.34	2.38	2.43	2.47	2.51	2.55	2.59	2.64	2.68	2.72	2.76	2.80	2.85	2.89	2.93	2.97
4	2.93	2.99	3.04	3.09	3.14	3.20	3.25	3.30	3.36	3.41	3.46	3.51	3.57	3.62	3.67	3.73
5	3.53	3.59	3.65	3.72	3.78	3.84	3.91	3.97	4.04	4.10	4.16	4.23	4.29	4.35	4.42	4.48
6	4.12	4.20	4.27	4.35	4.42	4.49	4.57	4.64	4.72	4.79	4.87	4.94	5.02	5.09	5.17	5.24
7	4.72	4.81	4.89	4.98	5.06	5.15	5.23	5.32	5.40	5.49	5.58	5.66	5.75	5.83	5.92	6.00
8	5.32	5.42	5.51	5.61	5.71	5.80	5.90	6.00	6.09	6.19	6.29	6.38	6.48	6.58	6.67	6.77
9	5.92	6.03	6.14	6.25	6.35	6.46	6.57	6.68	6.78	6.89	7.00	7.11	7.22	7.32	7.43	7.54
10	6.53	6.65	6.77	6.88	7.00	7.12	7.24	7.36	7.48	7.60	7.72	7.84	7.96	8.08	8.19	8.31
11	7.14	7.27	7.40	7.53	7.66	7.79	7.92	8.05	8.18	8.31	8.44	8.57	8.70	8.83	8.96	9.09
12	7.74	7.89	8.03	8.17	8.31	8.45	8.59	8.74	8.88	9.02	9.16	9.30	9.45	9.59	9.73	9.87
13	8.36	8.51	8.66	8.81	8.97	9.12	9.27	9.43	9.58	9.73	9.89	10.04	10.20	10.35	10.50	10.66
14	8.97	9.13	9.30	9.46	9.63	9.79	9.96	10.12	10.29	10.45	10.62	10.78	10.95	11.11	11.28	11.45
15	9.59	9.76	9.94	10.11	10.29	10.47	10.64	10.82	11.00	11.17	11.35	11.53	11.71	11.88	12.06	12.24
16	10.20	10.39	10.58	10.77	10.95	11.14	11.33	11.52	11.71	11.90	12.09	12.28	12.46	12.65	12.84	13.03
17	10.82	11.02	11.22	11.42	11.62	11.82	12.02	12.22	12.42	12.62	12.83	13.03	13.23	13.43	13.63	13.83
18	11.45	11.66	11.87	12.08	12.29	12.50	12.72	12.93	13.14	13.35	13.57	13.78	13.99	14.21	14.42	14.64
19	12.07	12.30	12.52	12.74	12.97	13.19	13.41	13.64	13.86	14.09	14.31	14.54	14.76	14.99	15.22	15.44
20	12.70	12.93	13.17	13.41	13.64	13.88	14.11	14.35	14.59	14.82	15.06	15.30	15.54	15.77	16.01	16.25
21	13.33	13.58	13.82	14.07	14.32	14.57	14.82	15.06	15.31	15.56	15.81	16.06	16.31	16.56	16.81	17.07
22	13.96	14.22	14.48	14.74	15.00	15.26	15.52	15.78	16.04	16.30	16.57	16.83	17.09	17.36	17.62	17.88
23	14.59	14.87	15.14	15.41	15.68	15.96	16.23	16.50	16.78	17.05	17.32	17.60	17.88	18.15	18.43	18.70
24	15.23	15.51	15.80	16.08	16.37	16.65	16.94	17.22	17.51	17.80	18.09	18.37	18.66	18.95	19.24	19.53
25	15.87	16.17	16.46	16.76	17.06	17.35	17.65	17.95	18.25	18.55	18.85	19.15	19.45	19.75	20.05	20.36
26	16.51	16.82	17.13	17.44	17.75	18.06	18.37	18.68	18.99	19.30	19.62	19.93	20.24	20.56	20.87	21.19
27	17.15	17.47	17.80	18.12	18.44	18.76	19.09	19.41	19.74	20.06	20.39	20.71	21.04	21.37	21.69	22.02
28	17.80	18.13	18.47	18.80	19.14	19.47	19.81	20.15	20.48	20.82	21.16	21.50	21.84	22.18	22.52	22.86
29	18.45	18.79	19.14	19.49	19.83	20.18	20.53	20.88	21.23	21.58	21.94	22.29	22.64	22.99	23.35	23.70
30	19.10	19.45	19.81	20.17	20.54	20.90	21.26	21.62	21.99	22.35	22.72	23.08	23.45	23.81	24.18	24.55
31	19.75	20.12	20.49	20.87	21.24	21.61	21.99	22.37	22.74	23.12	23.50	23.88	24.26	24.64	25.02	25.40
32	20.40	20.79	21.17	21.56	21.95	22.33	22.72	23.11	23.50	23.89	24.28	24.68	25.07	25.46	25.86	26.25
33	21.06	21.46	21.85	22.25	22.65	23.06	23.46	23.86	24.26	24.67	25.07	25.48	25.88	26.29	26.70	27.11
34	21.72	22.13	22.54	22.95	23.37	23.78	24.19	24.61	25.03	25.44	25.86	26.28	26.70	27.12	27.54	27.97
35	22.38	22.80	23.23	23.65	24.08	24.51	24.94	25.36	25.79	26.23	26.66	27.09	27.52	27.96	28.39	28.83
36	23.04	23.48	23.92	24.35	24.80	25.24	25.68	26.12	26.57	27.01	27.46	27.90	28.35	28.80	29.25	29.70
37	23.70	24.16	24.61	25.06	25.52	25.97	26.42	26.88	27.34	27.80	28.26	28.72	29.18	29.64	30.10	30.57
38	24.37	24.84	25.30	25.77	26.24	26.70	27.17	27.64	28.11	28.59	29.06	29.53	30.01	30.49	30.96	31.44
39	25.04	25.52	26.00	26.48	26.96	27.44	27.92	28.41	28.89	29.38	29.87	30.36	30.85	31.34	31.83	32.32
40	25.71	26.20	26.70	27.19	27.69	28.18	28.68	29.18	29.68	30.18	30.68	31.18	31.68	32.19	32.69	33.20
41	26.39	26.89	27.40	27.91	28.41	28.92	29.44	29.95	30.46	30.97	31.49	32.01	32.52	33.04	33.56	34.08
42	27.06	27.58	28.10	28.62	29.15	29.67	30.19	30.72	31.25	31.78	32.31	32.84	33.37	33.90	34.44	34.97
43	27.74	28.27	28.81	29.34	29.88	30.42	30.96	31.50	32.04	32.58	33.13	33.67	34.22	34.76	35.31	35.86
44	28.42	28.97	29.52	30.07	30.62	31.17	31.72	32.28	32.83	33.39	33.95	34.51	35.07	35.63	36.19	36.76
45	29.11	29.67	30.23	30.79	31.36	31.92	32.49	33.06	33.63	34.20	34.77	35.35	35.92	36.50	37.08	37.66
46	29.79	30.36	30.94	31.52	32.10	32.68	33.26	33.84	34.43	35.01	35.60	36.19	36.78	37.37	37.96	38.56
47	30.48	31.07	31.66	32.25	32.84	33.44	34.03	34.63	35.23	35.83	36.43	37.04	37.64	38.25	38.86	39.46
48	31.17	31.77	32.37	32.98	33.59	34.20	34.81	35.42	36.03	36.65	37.27	37.88	38.50	39.13	39.75	40.37
49	31.86	32.48	33.09	33.71	34.34	34.96	35.59	36.21	36.84	37.47	38.10	38.74	39.37	40.01	40.65	41.29
50	32.55	33.18	33.82	34.45	35.09	35.73	36.37	37.01	37.65	38.30	38.94	39.59	40.24	40.89	41.55	42.20
51	33.25	33.89	34.54	35.19	35.84	36.49	37.15	37.81	38.46	39.12	39.79	40.45	41.11	41.78	42.45	43.12
52	33.95	34.61	35.27	35.93	36.60	37.27	37.94	38.61	39.28	39.96	40.63	41.31	41.99	42.67	43.36	44.04
53	34.65	35.32	36.00	36.68	37.36	38.04	38.72	39.41	40.10	40.79	41.48	42.17	42.87	43.57	44.27	44.97
54	35.35	36.04	36.73	37.42	38.12	38.82	39.52	40.22	40.92	41.63	42.33	43.04	43.75	44.47	45.18	45.90
55	36.05	36.76	37.46	38.17	38.88	39.60	40.31	41.03	41.74	42.47	43.19	43.91	44.64	45.37	46.10	46.83
56	36.76	37.48	38.20	38.92	39.65	40.38	41.11	41.84	42.57	43.31	44.05	44.79	45.53	46.27	47.02	47.77
57	37.47	38.20	38.94	39.68	40.42	41.16	41.91	42.65	43.40	44.15	44.91	45.66	46.42	47.18	47.94	48.71
58	38.18	38.93	39.68	40.43	41.19	41.95	42.71	43.47	44.23	45.00	45.77	46.54	47.32	48.09	48.87	49.65
59	38.89	39.66	40.42	41.19	41.96	42.74	43.51	44.29	45.07	45.85	46.64	47.42	48.21	49.01	49.80	50.60
60	39.61	40.39	41.17	41.95	42.74	43.53	44.32	45.11	45.91	46.71	47.51	48.31	49.12	49.92	50.73	51.55

NUMBER OF PAYMENTS	18.00%	18.25%	18.50%	18.75%	19.00%	19.25%	19.50%	19.75%	20.00%	20.25%	20.50%	20.75%	21.00%	21.25%	21.50%	21.75%
					(FINANCE CHARGE PER $100 OF AMOUNT FINANCED)											
1	1.50	1.52	1.54	1.56	1.58	1.60	1.62	1.65	1.67	1.69	1.71	1.73	1.75	1.77	1.79	1.81
2	2.26	2.29	2.32	2.35	2.38	2.41	2.44	2.48	2.51	2.54	2.57	2.60	2.63	2.66	2.70	2.73
3	3.01	3.06	3.10	3.14	3.18	3.23	3.27	3.31	3.35	3.39	3.44	3.48	3.52	3.56	3.60	3.65
4	3.78	3.83	3.88	3.94	3.99	4.04	4.10	4.15	4.20	4.25	4.31	4.36	4.41	4.47	4.52	4.57
5	4.54	4.61	4.67	4.74	4.80	4.86	4.93	4.99	5.06	5.12	5.18	5.25	5.31	5.37	5.44	5.50
6	5.32	5.39	5.46	5.54	5.61	5.69	5.76	5.84	5.91	5.99	6.06	6.14	6.21	6.29	6.36	6.44
7	6.09	6.18	6.26	6.35	6.43	6.52	6.60	6.69	6.78	6.86	6.95	7.04	7.12	7.21	7.29	7.38
8	6.87	6.96	7.06	7.16	7.26	7.35	7.45	7.55	7.64	7.74	7.84	7.94	8.03	8.13	8.23	8.33
9	7.65	7.76	7.87	7.97	8.08	8.19	8.30	8.41	8.52	8.63	8.73	8.84	8.95	9.06	9.17	9.28
10	8.43	8.55	8.67	8.79	8.91	9.03	9.15	9.27	9.39	9.51	9.63	9.75	9.88	10.00	10.12	10.24
11	9.22	9.35	9.49	9.62	9.75	9.88	10.01	10.14	10.28	10.41	10.54	10.67	10.80	10.94	11.07	11.20
12	10.02	10.16	10.30	10.44	10.59	10.73	10.87	11.02	11.16	11.31	11.45	11.59	11.74	11.88	12.02	12.17
13	10.81	10.97	11.12	11.28	11.43	11.59	11.74	11.90	12.05	12.21	12.36	12.52	12.67	12.83	12.99	13.14
14	11.61	11.78	11.95	12.11	12.28	12.45	12.61	12.78	12.95	13.11	13.28	13.45	13.62	13.79	13.95	14.12
15	12.42	12.59	12.77	12.95	13.13	13.31	13.49	13.67	13.85	14.03	14.21	14.39	14.57	14.75	14.93	15.11
16	13.22	13.41	13.60	13.80	13.99	14.18	14.37	14.56	14.75	14.94	15.13	15.33	15.52	15.71	15.90	16.10
17	14.04	14.24	14.44	14.64	14.85	15.05	15.25	15.46	15.66	15.86	16.07	16.27	16.48	16.68	16.89	17.09
18	14.85	15.07	15.28	15.49	15.71	15.93	16.14	16.36	16.57	16.79	17.01	17.22	17.44	17.66	17.88	18.09
19	15.67	15.90	16.12	16.35	16.58	16.81	17.03	17.26	17.49	17.72	17.95	18.18	18.41	18.64	18.87	19.10
20	16.49	16.73	16.97	17.21	17.45	17.69	17.93	18.17	18.41	18.66	18.90	19.14	19.38	19.63	19.87	20.11
21	17.32	17.57	17.82	18.07	18.33	18.58	18.83	19.09	19.34	19.60	19.85	20.11	20.36	20.62	20.87	21.13
22	18.15	18.41	18.68	18.94	19.21	19.47	19.74	20.01	20.27	20.54	20.81	21.08	21.34	21.61	21.88	22.15
23	18.98	19.26	19.54	19.81	20.09	20.37	20.65	20.93	21.21	21.49	21.77	22.05	22.33	22.61	22.90	23.18
24	19.82	20.11	20.40	20.69	20.98	21.27	21.56	21.86	22.15	22.44	22.74	23.03	23.33	23.62	23.92	24.21
25	20.66	20.96	21.27	21.57	21.87	22.18	22.48	22.79	23.10	23.40	23.71	24.02	24.32	24.63	24.94	25.25
26	21.50	21.82	22.14	22.45	22.77	23.09	23.41	23.73	24.04	24.36	24.68	25.01	25.33	25.65	25.97	26.29
27	22.35	22.68	23.01	23.34	23.67	24.00	24.33	24.67	25.00	25.33	25.67	26.00	26.34	26.67	27.01	27.34
28	23.20	23.55	23.89	24.23	24.58	24.92	25.27	25.61	25.96	26.30	26.65	27.00	27.35	27.70	28.05	28.40
29	24.06	24.41	24.77	25.13	25.49	25.84	26.20	26.56	26.92	27.28	27.64	28.00	28.37	28.73	29.09	29.46
30	24.92	25.29	25.66	26.03	26.40	26.77	27.14	27.52	27.89	28.26	28.64	29.01	29.39	29.77	30.14	30.52
31	25.78	26.16	26.55	26.93	27.32	27.70	28.09	28.47	28.86	29.25	29.64	30.03	30.42	30.81	31.20	31.59
32	26.65	27.04	27.44	27.84	28.24	28.64	29.04	29.44	29.84	30.24	30.64	31.05	31.45	31.85	32.26	32.67
33	27.52	27.93	28.34	28.75	29.16	29.57	29.99	30.40	30.82	31.23	31.65	32.07	32.49	32.91	33.33	33.75
34	28.39	28.81	29.24	29.66	30.09	30.52	30.95	31.37	31.80	32.23	32.67	33.10	33.53	33.96	34.40	34.83
35	29.27	29.71	30.14	30.58	31.02	31.47	31.91	32.35	32.79	33.24	33.68	34.13	34.58	35.03	35.47	35.92
36	30.15	30.60	31.05	31.51	31.96	32.42	32.87	33.33	33.79	34.25	34.71	35.17	35.63	36.09	36.56	37.02
37	31.03	31.50	31.97	32.43	32.90	33.37	33.84	34.32	34.79	35.26	35.74	36.21	36.69	37.16	37.64	38.12
38	31.92	32.40	32.88	33.37	33.85	34.33	34.82	35.30	35.79	36.28	36.77	37.26	37.75	38.24	38.73	39.23
39	32.81	33.31	33.80	34.30	34.80	35.30	35.80	36.30	36.80	37.30	37.81	38.31	38.82	39.32	39.83	40.34
40	33.71	34.22	34.73	35.24	35.75	36.26	36.78	37.29	37.81	38.33	38.85	39.37	39.89	40.41	40.93	41.46
41	34.61	35.13	35.66	36.18	36.71	37.24	37.77	38.30	38.83	39.36	39.89	40.43	40.96	41.50	42.04	42.58
42	35.51	36.05	36.59	37.13	37.67	38.21	38.76	39.30	39.85	40.40	40.95	41.50	42.05	42.60	43.15	43.71
43	36.42	36.97	37.52	38.08	38.63	39.19	39.75	40.31	40.87	41.44	42.00	42.57	43.13	43.70	44.27	44.84
44	37.33	37.89	38.46	39.03	39.60	40.18	40.75	41.33	41.90	42.48	43.06	43.64	44.22	44.81	45.39	45.98
45	38.24	38.82	39.41	39.99	40.58	41.17	41.75	42.35	42.94	43.53	44.13	44.72	45.32	45.92	46.52	47.12
46	39.16	39.75	40.35	40.95	41.55	42.16	42.76	43.37	43.98	44.58	45.20	45.81	46.42	47.03	47.65	48.27
47	40.08	40.69	41.30	41.92	42.54	43.15	43.77	44.40	45.02	45.64	46.27	46.90	47.53	48.16	48.79	49.42
48	41.00	41.63	42.26	42.89	43.52	44.15	44.79	45.43	46.07	46.71	47.35	47.99	48.64	49.28	49.93	50.58
49	41.93	42.57	43.22	43.86	44.51	45.16	45.81	46.46	47.12	47.77	48.43	49.09	49.75	50.41	51.08	51.74
50	42.86	43.52	44.18	44.84	45.50	46.17	46.83	47.50	48.17	48.84	49.52	50.19	50.87	51.55	52.23	52.91
51	43.79	44.47	45.14	45.82	46.50	47.18	47.86	48.55	49.23	49.92	50.61	51.30	51.99	52.69	53.38	54.08
52	44.73	45.42	46.11	46.80	47.50	48.20	48.89	49.59	50.30	51.00	51.71	52.41	53.12	53.83	54.55	55.26
53	45.67	46.38	47.08	47.79	48.50	49.22	49.93	50.65	51.37	52.09	52.81	53.53	54.26	54.98	55.71	56.44
54	46.62	47.34	48.06	48.78	49.51	50.24	50.97	51.70	52.44	53.17	53.91	54.65	55.39	56.14	56.88	57.63
55	47.57	48.30	49.04	49.78	50.52	51.27	52.02	52.76	53.52	54.27	55.02	55.78	56.54	57.30	58.06	58.82
56	48.52	49.27	50.03	50.78	51.54	52.30	53.06	53.83	54.60	55.37	56.14	56.91	57.68	58.46	59.24	60.02
57	49.47	50.24	51.01	51.79	52.56	53.34	54.12	54.90	55.68	56.47	57.25	58.04	58.84	59.63	60.43	61.22
58	50.43	51.22	52.00	52.79	53.58	54.38	55.17	55.97	56.77	57.57	58.38	59.18	59.99	60.80	61.62	62.43
59	51.39	52.20	53.00	53.80	54.61	55.42	56.23	57.05	57.87	58.68	59.51	60.33	61.15	61.98	62.81	63.64
60	52.36	53.18	54.00	54.82	55.64	56.47	57.30	58.13	58.96	59.80	60.64	61.48	62.32	63.17	64.01	64.86

LIFE INSURANCE RATES FOR MALES (FOR FEMALES SUBTRACT 3 YEARS)*

Age	Five-year term	Age	Straight life	Age	Twenty-payment life	Age	Twenty-year endowment
20	1.85	20	5.90	20	8.28	20	13.85
21	1.85	21	6.13	21	8.61	21	14.35
22	1.85	22	6.35	22	8.91	22	14.92
23	1.85	23	6.60	23	9.23	23	15.54
24	1.85	24	6.85	24	9.56	24	16.05
25	1.85	25	7.13	25	9.91	25	17.55
26	1.85	26	7.43	26	10.29	26	17.66
27	1.86	27	7.75	27	10.70	27	18.33
28	1.86	28	8.08	28	11.12	28	19.12
29	1.87	29	8.46	29	11.58	29	20.00
30	1.87	30	8.85	30	12.05	30	20.90
31	1.87	31	9.27	31	12.57	31	21.88
32	1.88	32	9.71	32	13.10	32	22.89
33	1.95	33	10.20	33	13.67	33	23.98
34	2.08	34	10.71	34	14.28	34	25.13
35	2.23	35	11.26	35	14.92	35	26.35
36	2.44	36	11.84	36	15.60	36	27.64
37	2.67	37	12.46	37	16.30	37	28.97
38	2.95	38	13.12	38	17.04	38	30.38
39	3.24	39	13.81	39	17.81	39	31.84
40	3.52	40	14.54	40	18.61	40	33.36
41	3.79	41	15.30	41	19.44	41	34.94
42	4.04	42	16.11	42	20.31	42	36.59
43	4.26	43	16.96	43	21.21	43	38.29
44	4.50	44	17.86	44	22.15	44	40.09

*Note these tables are a sampling of age groups, premium costs, and insurance coverage that are available over 44 years of age.

NONFORFEITURE OPTIONS BASED ON $1,000 FACE VALUE

Years insurance policy in force	Straight life					Twenty-payment life					Twenty-year endowment			
	Cash value	Amount of paid-up insurance	Extended term		Cash value	Amount of paid-up insurance	Extended term		Cash value	Amount of paid-up insurance	Extended term	
			Years	Day			Years	Day			Years	Day
5	29	86	9	91	71	220	19	190	92	229	23	140
10	96	259	18	76	186	521	28	195	319	520	30	160
15	148	371	20	165	317	781	32	176	610	790	35	300
20	265	550	21	300	475	1,000	Life		1,000	1,000	Life	

COMPULSORY INSURANCE (BASED ON CLASS OF DRIVER)

Bodily injury to others		Damage to someone else's property	
Class	10/20	Class	5M
10	$ 55	10	129
17	98	17	160
18	80	18	160
20	116	20	186

DAMAGE TO SOMEONE ELSE'S PROPERTY

Class	10M	25M	50M	100M
10	132	134	135	136
17	164	166	168	169
18	164	166	168	169
20	191	193	195	197

TOWING AND SUBSTITUTE TRANSPORATION

Towing and labor	$ 4
Substitute transportation	16

FIRE INSURANCE RATES PER $100 OF COVERAGE FOR BUILDINGS AND CONTENTS

Rating of area	Classification of building			
	Class A		Class B	
	Buildings	Contents	Buildings	Contents
1	.28	.35	.41	.54
2	.33	.47	.50	.60
3	.41	.50	.61	.65

FIRE INSURANCE SHORT-RATE AND CANCELLATION TABLE

Time policy in force	Percent of annual rate to be charged	Time policy in force	Percent of annual rate to be charged	Time policy in force	Percent of annual rate to be charged
Days: 5	8%	Months: 3	35	Months: 8	74
10	10	4	44	9	81
20	15	5	52	10	87
25	17	6	61	11	96
Months: 1	19	7	67	12	100
2	27				

BODILY INJURY

Class	15/30	20/40	20/50	25/50	25/60	50/100	100/300	250/500	500/1000
10	27	37	40	44	47	69	94	144	187
17	37	52	58	63	69	104	146	228	298
18	33	46	50	55	60	89	124	193	251
20	41	59	65	72	78	119	168	263	344

COLLISION

Classes	Age group	Symbols 1–3 $300 ded.	Symbol 4 $300 ded.	Symbol 5 $300 ded.	Symbol 6 $300 ded.	Symbol 7 $300 ded.	Symbol 8 $300 ded.	Symbol 10 $300 ded.
10–20	1	180	180	187	194	214	264	279
	2	160	160	166	172	190	233	246
	3	148	148	154	166	183	221	233
	4	136	136	142	160	176	208	221
	5	124	124	130	154	169	196	208

Class	Additional cost to reduce deductible	
	From $300 to $200	From $300 to $100
10	13	27
17	20	43
18	16	33
20	26	55

COMPREHENSIVE

Classes	Age group	Symbols 1–3 $300 ded.	Symbol 4 $300 ded.	Symbol 5 $300 ded.	Symbol 6 $300 ded.	Symbol 7 $300 ded.	Symbol 8 $300 ded.	Symbol 10 $300 ded.
10–25	1	61	61	65	85	123	157	211
	2	55	55	58	75	108	138	185
	3	52	52	55	73	104	131	178
	4	49	49	52	70	99	124	170
	5	47	47	49	67	94	116	163

Additional cost to reduce deductible: From $300 to $200 add $4

LOAN AMORTIZATION TABLE (MONTHLY PAYMENT PER $1,000 TO PAY PRINCIPAL AND INTEREST ON INSTALLMENT LOAN)

Terms in months	7.50%	8%	8.50%	9%	10.00%	10.50%	11.00%	11.50%	12.00%
6	$170.34	$170.58	$170.83	$171.20	$171.56	$171.81	$172.05	$172.30	$172.55
12	86.76	86.99	87.22	87.46	87.92	88.15	88.38	88.62	88.85
18	58.92	59.15	59.37	59.60	60.06	60.29	60.52	60.75	60.98
24	45.00	45.23	45.46	45.69	46.14	46.38	46.61	46.84	47.07
30	36.66	36.89	37.12	37.35	37.81	38.04	38.28	38.51	38.75
36	31.11	31.34	31.57	31.80	32.27	32.50	32.74	32.98	33.21
42	27.15	27.38	27.62	27.85	28.32	28.55	28.79	29.03	29.28
48	24.18	24.42	24.65	24.77	25.36	25.60	25.85	26.09	26.33
54	21.88	22.12	22.36	22.59	23.07	23.32	23.56	23.81	24.06
60	20.04	20.28	20.52	20.76	21.25	21.49	21.74	21.99	22.24

Terms in months	12.50%	13.00%	13.50%	14.00%	14.50%	15.00%	15.50%	16.00%
6	$172.80	$173.04	$173.29	$173.54	$173.79	$174.03	$174.28	$174.53
12	89.08	89.32	89.55	89.79	90.02	90.26	90.49	90.73
18	61.21	61.45	61.68	61.92	62.15	62.38	62.62	62.86
24	47.31	47.54	47.78	48.01	48.25	48.49	48.72	48.96
30	38.98	39.22	39.46	39.70	39.94	40.18	40.42	40.66
36	33.45	33.69	33.94	34.18	34.42	34.67	34.91	35.16
42	29.52	29.76	30.01	30.25	30.50	30.75	31.00	31.25
48	26.58	26.83	27.08	27.33	27.58	27.83	28.08	28.34
54	24.31	24.56	24.81	25.06	25.32	25.58	25.84	26.10
60	22.50	22.75	23.01	23.27	23.53	23.79	24.05	24.32

AMORTIZATION CHART (MORTGAGE PRINCIPAL AND INTEREST PER THOUSAND DOLLARS)

Term in years	INTEREST												
	5%	$5\frac{1}{2}$%	6%	$6\frac{1}{2}$%	7%	$7\frac{1}{2}$%	8%	8 %	9%	$9\frac{1}{2}$%	10%	$10\frac{1}{2}$%	11%
10	10.61	10.86	11.11	11.36	11.62	11.88	12.14	12.40	12.67	12.94	13.22	13.50	13.78
12	9.25	9.51	9.76	10.02	10.29	10.56	10.83	11.11	11.39	11.67	11.96	12.25	12.54
15	7.91	8.18	8.44	8.72	8.99	9.28	9.56	9.85	10.15	10.45	10.75	11.06	11.37
17	7.29	7.56	7.84	8.12	8.40	8.69	8.99	9.29	9.59	9.90	10.22	10.54	10.86
20	6.60	6.88	7.17	7.46	7.76	8.06	8.37	8.68	9.00	9.33	9.66	9.99	10.33
22	6.20	6.51	6.82	7.13	7.44	7.75	8.07	8.39	8.72	9.05	9.39	9.73	10.08
25	5.85	6.15	6.45	6.76	7.07	7.39	7.72	8.06	8.40	8.74	9.09	9.45	9.81
30	5.37	5.68	6.00	6.33	6.66	7.00	7.34	7.69	8.05	8.41	8.78	9.15	9.53
35	5.05	5.38	5.71	6.05	6.39	6.75	7.11	7.47	7.84	8.22	8.60	8.99	9.37

Term in years	INTEREST												
	$11\frac{1}{2}$%	$11\frac{3}{4}$%	12%	$12\frac{1}{2}$%	$12\frac{3}{4}$%	13%	$13\frac{1}{2}$%	$13\frac{3}{4}$%	14%	$14\frac{1}{2}$%	$14\frac{3}{4}$%	15%	$15\frac{1}{2}$%
10	14.06	14.21	14.35	14.64	14.79	14.94	15.23	15.38	15.53	15.83	15.99	16.14	16.45
12	12.84	12.99	13.14	13.44	13.60	13.75	14.06	14.22	14.38	14.69	14.85	15.01	15.34
15	11.69	11.85	12.01	12.33	12.49	12.66	12.99	13.15	13.32	13.66	13.83	14.00	14.34
17	11.19	11.35	11.52	11.85	12.02	12.19	12.53	12.71	12.88	13.23	13.41	13.58	13.94
20	10.67	10.84	11.02	11.37	11.54	11.72	12.08	12.26	12.44	12.80	12.99	13.17	13.54
22	10.43	10.61	10.78	11.14	11.33	11.51	11.87	12.06	12.24	12.62	12.81	12.99	13.37
25	10.17	10.35	10.54	10.91	11.10	11.28	11.66	11.85	12.04	12.43	12.62	12.81	13.20
30	9.91	10.10	10.29	10.68	10.87	11.07	11.46	11.66	11.85	12.25	12.45	12.65	13.05
35	9.77	9.96	10.16	10.56	10.76	10.96	11.36	11.56	11.76	12.17	12.37	12.57	12.98

CHAPTER 1

Self-Paced Worksheet

Cover the answers on the right and fill in each blank. After answering the question, look to the right for your answer.

Vocabulary Review

1. The _____ _____ place-value chart divides groups of three digits right to left by units, thousands, millions, billions, and trillions.
2. The total in the adding process is called the _____.
3. The smaller number that is being subtracted from another is called the _____.
4. The answer from a subtraction problem is the _____.
5. Numbers that are combined in the addition process are called _____.
6. Multiplicand times multiplier equals the _____.
7. The _____ is the number in the division process that is dividing into another.
8. The _____ is the leftover amount in the division process.
9. _____ _____ _____ _____ results in only one nonzero digit left. This means rounding to first digit of number.
10. The _____ is the answer of a division problem.

Theory Tips (and/or Cautions)

11. The 5 in 7,853 is in the _____ place.
12. The 4 in 64,115,328 is in the _____ place.
13. In rounding 1,456 to the nearest thousands, the first step is to identify the _____ _____ of the digit you want to round.
14. In rounding, if digit to right of identified digit is _____ or greater, identified digit is increased by one.
15. Rounding all the way results in only _____ _____ digit remaining.
16. The first step in dissecting a word problem is to _____ _____ _____.
17. Adding of whole numbers is done _____ to _____.

18. The difference plus the subtrahend equals the _____.
19. The numbers between the multiplier and the product are _____ _____.
20. We can _____ the multiplication process by reversing the multiplicand and multiplier and then multiplying.
21. $75,000 \times 20$ is completed by multiplying 75×2 and _____ _____ zeros to answer.
22. The divisor times quotient plus remainder equals the _____.
23. $66,000 \div 100$ results in dropping _____ zeros in the dividend.

Calculations/Applications

Do calculations on scrap paper as needed. Worked-out solutions are provided at end.
24. Write in verbal the whole number 8,593 and illustrate place values.

25. Round 9,852 to nearest hundred.
26. Round 62,555 to nearest thousand.
27. Round 6,853 all the way.
28. Estimate by rounding all the way and then do actual calculation.
    6,666
    7,500
    7,215

	Answers
1.	whole number
2.	sum
3.	subtrahend
4.	difference
5.	addends
6.	product
7.	divisor
8.	remainder
9.	rounding all the way
10.	quotient
11.	tens
12.	millions
13.	place value
14.	five
15.	one nonzero
16.	gather the facts
17.	top bottom
18.	minuend
19.	partial products
20.	check
21.	adding (affixing) four
22.	dividend
23.	two
24.	eight thousand, five hundred ninety-three $(8 \times 1,000) + (5 \times 100) + (9 \times 10) + (3 \times 1)$
25.	9,900
26.	63,000
27.	7,000
28.	22,000 est. 21,381

29. Subtract: 9,432
                 −3,618

30. Multiply 86 × 1,000 by the shortcut method.

31. Multiply 751 (do not multiply rows of zeros).
                406

32. Divide 7,041 ÷ 128 and show any remainder.

33. Divide 99,000 ÷ 100 by the shortcut method.

34. Chrysler produces 650 vans each workday (Monday through Friday). If the cost to produce each car is $7,000, what is Chrysler's cost for the year?

29. 5,814

30. 86,000
31. 304,906

32. 55 Rem 1
33. 990
34. $1,183,000,000

Worked-Out Solutions to Calculations/Applications Section

25. 9,852 → 9,900
        ↑

26. 62,555 → 63,000
        ↑

27. 6,853 → 7,000
        ↑

28. 6,666 → 7,000
         7,500 → 8,000
         7,215 → 7,000
        21,381   22,000

29. 8 14 2 12
         9,4 3 2
         3,6 1 8
         5,8 1 4

30. 86 + 3 zeros

31.   751
             406
            4506
           30040
           304,906

32.   55 Rem1
           128)7041
               640
               641
               640
                 1

33. 99,000 = 990

34.   5 × 650 = 3,250
          3,250 × 52 = 169,000
      169,000 × $7,000 = $1,183,000,000

Word Problem Practice Quiz

Check with your instructor for complete worked-out solutions.

1–1. Mel Jones received the following grades in a computer science class: 90, 70, 50, 85, 75, and 60. The instructor said he would drop the lowest grade. What is Mel's average?

1–2. Judy Small had a $850 balance in her checkbook. During the week, she wrote checks for rent, $180; telephone, $60; food, $95; and entertaining $45. She also made a deposit of $1,200. Calculate the new checkbook balance.

1–3. James Company carpeted its offices requiring 711 square yards of commercial carpet. The total cost of the carpet was $3,555. How much did James pay per square yard?

1–4. The Angel Company produced 26,580 cans of paint in August. Angel was able to sell 21,946 of these cans. Calculate ending inventory of paint cans along with its total inventory cost assuming each can cost $12.

1–5. A computer with a regular price of $4,500 was reduced by $1,255. Calculate the new selling price of the computer. Assuming 900 customers purchased the computer, what were the sales to the store?

1–6. Mills Hardware on Monday sold 40 rakes at $7 each, 8 wrenches at $5 each, 10 bags of grass seed at $6 each, 9 lawn mowers at $205 each, and 33 cans of paint at $4 each. What were the total dollar sales for Mills on Monday?

1–7. Dick Herch, a college editor, was going on a business trip that would take him from Boston (starting point) to New York and to Washington, D.C. Dick estimated he would be traveling 1,901 miles round trip. In actuality, the drive from Boston to New York was 228 miles, and from New York to Washington, D.C. was 242 miles. Calculate how many miles Dick overestimated his trip.

1–8. Jay Miller loves to ski. He rents a ski chalet for $1,350 per month for 4 months. What is Jay's rental charge for the 4 months? Assume Jay spends $6,250 for the total trip. How much did he spend above the renting of the ski chalet?

1–9. Jill Rite borrowed $20,000 to buy a new car. Assume a finance charge of $4,900. What will be her monthly payment if she takes 60 months to repay the loan (plus finance charge)? Assume the loan is repaid in equal payments.

1–10. Jim Rose bought 7,000 shares of stock in the Flight Company. After holding the stock for 6 months, he sold 400 shares on Monday, 330 shares on Tuesday and again on Thursday, and 800 shares on Friday. Calculate the total number of shares Jim still has. If the average share of stock is worth $39 per share, what is the total value of his stock?

CHAPTER 2

Self-Paced Worksheet

Cover the answers on the right and fill in each blank. After answering the question, look to the right for your answer.

Vocabulary Review

1. Like fractions are _____ _____ with the same denominators.
2. _____ is the reducing process to simplify multiplication and division of fractions.
3. A fraction reaches its _____ _____ when no number divides evenly into the numerator and denominator except the number 1.
4. $\frac{7}{5}$, of which 5 is called the _____.
5. A _____ _____ (larger than 1) is only divisible by itself and one.
6. The _____ _____ _____ is the smallest nonzero whole number into which all denominators will divide evenly.
7. The _____ _____ _____ is the largest possible number that will divide evenly into both the numerator and denominator.
8. The _____ of a fraction is the interchanging of the numerator and denominator.
9. An _____ _____ is when the numerator is equal to or greater than the denominator.
10. _____ _____ are proper fractions with different denominators.

1.	proper fractions
2.	cancellation
3.	lowest terms
4.	denominator
5.	prime number
6.	least common denominator
7.	greatest common divisor
8.	reciprocal
9.	improper fraction
10.	unlike fractions

Theory Tips (and/or Cautions)

11. When converting an improper fraction to a mixed number, the remainder will be placed over the _____ denominator.
12. When converting mixed numbers to improper fractions, the _____ will stay the same.
13. The greatest common divisor cannot be a _____.
14. Dividing numerator and denominator by the greatest common divisor will result in reducing the fraction to its _____ _____.
15. The _____ _____ you use is the greatest common divisor when using the step approach.
16. $\frac{2}{7}$ or $\frac{8}{28}$ are _____ in value.
17. In adding or subtracting fractions, they should be _____ _____ _____ terms.
18. In adding or subtracting fractions with different denominators, the _____ _____ _____ must be found.
19. In finding the LCD by prime numbers, the next highest prime number will be used if smaller prime number will not divide evenly into at least _____ numbers.
20. When borrowing _____ from a whole number where subtracting in a mixed number problem, it has the same value as $\frac{5}{5}$ or $\frac{4}{4}$.
21. $\frac{4}{1}$ is equal to _____.
22. If cancellation is not used in the multiplying of mixed numbers the answer may have to be _____ _____ _____ _____.
23. 5 and $\frac{1}{5}$ are _____. When these two numbers are multiplied, they equal 1.
24. If your answer is an _____ _____ be sure to reduce it to lowest terms.

11.	old
12.	denominator
13.	zero
14.	lowest terms
15.	last divisor
16.	equivalent
17.	reduced to lowest
18.	least common denominator
19.	two
20.	1
21.	4
22.	reduced to lowest terms
23.	reciprocals
24.	improper fraction

Calculations/Applications

Do calculations on scrap paper as needed. Worked-out solutions are provided at end.

25. Convert to mixed number: $\frac{150}{7}$
26. Convert to an improper fraction: $9\frac{5}{8}$
27. Find the GCD by step approach and reduce to lowest terms: $\frac{15}{80}$
28. Convert to higher terms: $\frac{7}{10} = \frac{}{90}$

25.	$21\frac{3}{7}$
26.	$\frac{77}{8}$
27.	$5; \frac{3}{16}$
28.	$\frac{63}{90}$

29. Find the LCD: 15 6 3 4 2
30. Subtract: $8\frac{1}{8} - 6\frac{7}{24}$
31. Multiply (use cancelling): $14 \times \frac{2}{7}$
32. Multiply (do not use cancelling; reduce by GCD): $\frac{7}{8} \times \frac{6}{9}$
33. Complete: $\frac{1}{4} \div \frac{3}{6}$
34. A recent testing survey showed $\frac{1}{4}$ of all people surveyed preferred baking soda toothpaste to regular. If 26,000 people were in the survey, how many favored regular toothpaste? How many favored baking soda toothpaste?

29.	60
30.	$1\frac{5}{6}$
31.	4
32.	$\frac{7}{12}$
33.	$\frac{1}{2}$
34.	19,500
	6,500

Worked-Out Solutions to Calculations/Applications Section

25.
$$7\overline{)150} = 21\frac{3}{7}$$
$$\begin{array}{r} 21 \\ \underline{14} \\ 10 \\ \underline{7} \\ 3 \end{array}$$

26. $9\frac{5}{8} = \frac{72 + 5}{8} = \frac{77}{8}$

27.
$$15\overline{)80} \quad \text{⑤}\overline{)15} \quad \frac{15 \div 5}{80 \div 5} = \frac{3}{16}$$
$$\begin{array}{r} 5 \\ \underline{75} \\ 5 \end{array} \quad \begin{array}{r} 3 \\ \underline{15} \end{array}$$

28. $\frac{7}{10} = \frac{63}{90} \leftarrow (9 \times 7)$

29.
$$\begin{array}{r} 2\,\underline{|15\ \ 6\ \ 3\ \ 4\ \ 2} \\ 3\,\underline{|15\ \ 3\ \ 3\ \ 2\ \ 1} \\ 5\ \ 1\ \ 1\ \ 2\ \ 1 \end{array}$$
$$2 \times 3 \times 5 \times 1 \times 1 \times 2 \times 1 = 60$$

30.
$$\begin{array}{r} 8\frac{1}{8} = 8\frac{3}{24} = 7\frac{27}{24} \\ -6\frac{7}{24} - 6\frac{7}{24} = 6\frac{7}{24} \\ \hline = 1\frac{20}{24} = 1\frac{5}{6} \end{array}$$

31. $\overset{2}{\cancel{14}} \times \dfrac{2}{\underset{1}{\cancel{7}}} = 4$

32. $\dfrac{7}{8} \times \dfrac{6}{9} = \dfrac{42}{72}$
$$42\overline{)72} \quad 30\overline{)42} \quad 12\overline{)30} \quad 6\overline{)12}$$
$$\begin{array}{r} 1 \\ \underline{42} \\ 30 \end{array} \quad \begin{array}{r} 1 \\ \underline{30} \\ 12 \end{array} \quad \begin{array}{r} 2 \\ \underline{24} \\ 6 \end{array} \quad \begin{array}{r} 2 \\ \underline{12} \end{array}$$
$$\frac{42 \div 6}{72 \div 6} = \frac{7}{12}$$

33. $\dfrac{1}{\underset{2}{\cancel{4}}} \times \dfrac{\overset{\overset{1}{\cancel{3}}}{\cancel{6}}}{\underset{1}{\cancel{8}}} = \dfrac{1}{2}$

34. $\dfrac{3}{4} \times 26{,}000 = 19{,}500$

$\dfrac{1}{4} \times 26{,}000 = 6{,}500$

Word Problem Practice Quiz

Check with your instructor for complete worked-out solutions.

2–1. A survey conducted by a marketing class found that $\frac{7}{8}$ of all people surveyed favored digital watches over traditional styles. If 3,200 responded to the survey, how many actually favored using traditional watches?

2–2. Jack, Alice, and Frank entered into a partnership. Jack owns $\frac{1}{5}$ of the company and Alice owns $\frac{1}{8}$. Calculate what part is owned by Frank.

2–3. Bob Campbell, who loves to cook, makes an apple pie (serves 6) for his family. The recipe calls for $3\frac{1}{2}$ cups of apples,

$2\frac{3}{4}$ cups of flour, $\frac{1}{8}$ cup of margarine, $2\frac{1}{8}$ cups of sugar, and 5 eggs. Since guests are coming, he would like to make this pie to serve 24. How much of each ingredient should Bob use?

2–4. A trip from Boston to the White Mountains of New Hampshire will take $2\frac{7}{8}$ hours. Assume we are $\frac{1}{7}$ of the way there. How much longer will the trip take?

2–5. The price of a new van has increased by $\frac{2}{5}$. If the original price of the van was $15,000, what is the new price today?

2–6. Jim Smith felled a tree that was 120 feet long. Jim decided to cut the tree into pieces of $2\frac{1}{2}$ feet. How many pieces can be cut from this tree?

2–7. In 2004, the price of a Land Rover increased by $1\frac{1}{4}$ times the 2003 price of $38,000. What is the 2004 price?

2–8. During the winter, Bill Blank has been quite concerned about the total number of gallons of home heating fuel he used. Last winter he used $1,505\frac{7}{8}$ gallons of oil. Here is a summary of this year's usage. Is it more or less than the previous year? Also, how much more or less?

December	$525\frac{1}{4}$	February	$481\frac{3}{8}$
January	$488\frac{5}{8}$	March	$255\frac{1}{3}$

2–9. John Toby is paid $70 per day. John became ill on Monday and had to leave after $\frac{3}{7}$ of a day. What did he earn on Monday? (Assume no work, no pay).

2–10. Evan Summers bought $1\frac{3}{8}$ pounds of roast beef, $4\frac{5}{7}$ pounds of sliced cheese, and $\frac{3}{5}$ of a pound of coleslaw. What is the total weight of his purchases?

CHAPTER 3

Self-Paced Worksheet

Cover the answers on the right and fill in each blank. After answering the question, look to the right for your answer.

Vocabulary Review

1. The position located between units and tenths is called the _____ _____.
2. _____ are numbers written with digits to right of the decimal point.
3. A _____ _____ is a fraction with a denominator that has a power of 10.
4. A _____ _____ has no whole number(s) to left of the decimal point.
5. A _____ _____ is a combination of a whole number and a decimal.
6. Decimal numbers that repeat themselves continuously are called _____ _____.

1. decimal point
2. decimals
3. decimal fraction
4. pure decimal
5. mixed decimal
6. repeating decimals

Theory Tips (and/or Cautions)

7. 4.53918 The 1 is in the _____ _____ place value.
8. In rounding decimals, drop _____ _____ to right of the identified digit.
9. .8, .80, .800 all have the same _____.
10. .33$\overline{3}$ is an example of a _____ decimal.
11. 3.0, 3.000, 3.0000 all have the same _____.
12. If the total number of places is greater than there are places in the product (from multiplying decimals), insert _____ in front of the product.
13. The _____ does not change when we multiply the divisor and dividend by the same number.
14. When multiplying decimals by multiples of 10, the answers are _____ than the original number.
15. When dividing decimals by multiples of 10, the answers are _____ than the original number.

7. ten thousandths
8. all digits
9. value
10. repeating
11. value
12. zeros
13. quotient
14. larger
15. smaller

Calculations/Applications

Do calculations on scrap paper as needed. Worked-out solutions are provided at end.

16. .3333 rounded to nearest thousandths is _____.
17. .16593 rounded to nearest hundredth is _____.
18. Convert to a decimal: $\frac{88}{100,000}$
19. .713 converted to a decimal fraction is _____.
20. .07$\frac{1}{4}$ converted to a decimal fraction is _____.
21. $\frac{1}{6}$ converted to decimal is _____ (round to nearest hundredth).
22. Rearrange vertically and add: 4.1, 14.82, 16.321
23. Multiply and round to nearest hundredth: 15.41 × 18.8
24. Divide and round to nearest hundredth: 3,142 ÷ 3.91
25. Complete by shortcut method: 4,138 ÷ 10,000
26. At Hertz, the cost per day to rent a full-size car is $49.99, plus $.18 per mile. What is the charge to rent this car for 2 days if you drove 959.8 miles?
27. A $2,800 computer would cost how much in Canada? (Use table in *Business Math Handbook;* round to nearest cent.)

16. .333
17. .17
18. .00088
19. $\frac{713}{1,000}$
20. $\frac{725}{10,000}$
21. .17
22. 35.241
23. 289.71
24. 803.58
25. .4138
26. $272.74
27. $3,661.00

Worked-Out Solutions to Calculations/Applications Section

16. .33$\underset{\uparrow}{3}$3 → .333

17. .1$\underset{\uparrow}{6}$593 → .17

18. $\frac{88}{100,000}$ ← .00088
    5 places

19. $\frac{713}{1,000}$ (1 + 3 places)

20. $.07\frac{1}{4} \rightarrow$
$$\begin{array}{r} .07 \\ +.0025 \\ \hline .0725 \rightarrow \dfrac{725}{1+4 \text{ places}} = \dfrac{725}{10,000} \end{array}$$

21. $\dfrac{1}{6} = .16\overset{\uparrow}{6} = .17$

22.
$$\begin{array}{r} 4.100 \\ 14.820 \\ 16.321 \\ \hline 35.241 \end{array}$$

23.
$$\begin{array}{r} 1\,5.4\,1 \\ \times\,1\,8.8 \\ \hline 1\,2\,3\,2\,8 \\ 1\,2\,3\,2\,8 \\ 1\,5\,4\,1 \\ \hline 2\,8\,9\underset{\uparrow}{7}0\,8 \rightarrow 289.708 \rightarrow 289.71 \end{array}$$

24.
$$\begin{array}{r} 803.580 \\ 3.91\overline{)314200.000} \rightarrow 803.58 \\ 3128 \\ \hline 1400 \\ 1173 \\ \hline 2270 \\ 1955 \\ \hline 3150 \\ 3128 \\ \hline 220 \end{array}$$

25. $.41\overset{\frown}{38} \rightarrow .4138$

26.
$$\begin{array}{r} \$49.99 \times 2 \;\; = \$ \; 99.98 \\ \$.18 \times 959.8 = \;\;\underline{172.76} \\ \text{Total charge} \; = \$272.74 \end{array}$$

27. $\$2,800 \times 1.3075 = \$3,661.00$

Word Problem Practice Quiz

Check with your instructor for complete worked-out solutions.
Round where applicable to nearest hundredth.

3–1. Bob Baker bought season tickets to a professional basketball team's games. The cost was $795.88. The package included 38 home games. What is the average price of the tickets per game? Round to nearest cent. Jim has requested to buy 4 of the tickets from Bob. What will be the total price Bob should receive?

3–2. The level of the oil tank in Henry's basement at the beginning of January read 310.75 gallons. During the month it was filled with 112.85 gallons. Henry used 125.95 gallons in January. What is the number of gallons of oil that Henry has to begin February?

3–3. Printed pencils cost $.08\overline{3}$ each for an order of 144,000 pencils. On Monday, Jim Company placed an order for the 144,000 pencils. What is the cost of the pencils for Jim Company? (Hint: Use the fractional equivalent in your calculation.)

3–4. Irene was shopping for corn beef at Market A; it was $2.158 per pound. At Market B, corn beef was $2.06 per pound. How much cheaper is Market B?

3–5. Shelley Scupper bought a new sweater for $101.88. She gave the salesperson two $100 bills. what is Shelley's change?

3–6. Joe is traveling to a convention by car. His company will reimburse him $.34 per mile.

Assume Joe traveled 1,011.8 miles. What reimbursement can he expect?

3–7. Morris Katz bought 4 new tires for his car at $129.35 per tire. He was also charged $3.15 per tire for mounting, $2.80 per tire for valve cores, and $4.95 per tire for balancing. Assuming no tax, what did Morris really pay for those 4 tires?

3–8. Alice wants to put wall-to-wall carpeting in her house. She will need 108.7 yards for downstairs, 19.8 yards for halls, and 175.9 yards for the upstairs bedrooms. She chose a shag carpet that costs $14.95 per yard. Alice also ordered foam padding at $3.25 per year. The installers quoted Alice a labor cost of $6.10 per yard in installation. What will the total job cost Alice?

3–9. A trip to Mexico costs 4,900 pesos. How much would this be in U.S. dollars? Check your answer.

3–10. The normal winter snowfall is 129.55 inches for Jordan County. this winter, the following snowfall resulted:

	Inches
December	29.33
January	44.453
February	18.85
March	16.35

What was this winter's total snowfall? How much was the snowfall above or below normal?

CHAPTER 4

Self-Paced Worksheet

Cover the answers on the right and fill in each blank. After answering the question, look to the right for your answer.

Vocabulary Review:

1. _____ _____ is the process of comparing the bank balance to the checkbook balance.

2. A record-keeping device called a _____ _____ records checks paid and deposits made by companies using a checking account.

3. A _____ _____ provides a record of checks written.

4. A _____ _____ identifies the next person or company to whom the check is to be transferred.

5. The _____ is the one who is named to receive the amount of the check.

6. Credit card sales less returns equal _____ _____.

7. A _____ memo indicates what a bank is adding to your account.

8. One who writes the check is called the _____.

9. _____ _____ _____ are deposits not received or processed by the bank at the time the bank statement is prepared.

10. Checks written but not yet processed by the bank before the bank statement preparation are called _____ _____.

1. bank reconciliation
2. check register
3. check stub
4. full endorsement
5. payee
6. net deposits
7. credit
8. drawer
9. deposits in transit
10. outstanding checks

Theory Tips (and/or Cautions)

11. If the verbal amount on a check doesn't match the figure amount, the bank by law uses the _____ amount.

12. _____ _____ can be further endorsed by someone who receives it intentionally or through loss.

13. A _____ _____ means the bank is decreasing one's account.

14. _____ is an important cause of differences between bank and checkbook.

15. An NSF will result in the bank _____ one's checkbook balance.

16. In the reconciliation process, deposits in transit and outstanding checks affect the _____ balance.

17. If the bank statement shows a note collected, the checkbook balance in the reconciliation process will be _____.

18. If a $20 check was recorded as $10, we need to lower the _____ balance by another $10.

19. Interest earned on a checking account will be _____ to one's account.

20. ATM cards are _____ cards.

21. Check stubs should be _____ before the check is written.

11. verbal
12. blank endorsement
13. debit memorandum
14. timing
15. lowering
16. bank
17. increased
18. checkbook
19. credited
20. debit
21. completed

Calculations/Applications

Do calculations on scrap paper as needed. Worked-out solutions are provided at end.

22. Given the following from the check register, calculate the ending balance.

Beginning balance		$481.92
Payment	$ 81.22	
Payment	19.44	
Deposit	111.22	
Payment	88.04	

22. $404.44

52

23. Calculate the net deposit from the following:

Credit card sales	Credit card returns
$ 15.88	$ 12.88
108.44	142.80
339.40	

23. $308.04

24. Write the following amount in verbal form as you would on a check: $675.88

24. Six hundred seventy-five and 88/100

25. Calculate reconciled bank balance, given the following:

Bank statement balance	$4,800.10
Checks outstanding	55.32
Deposits in transit	105.99

25. $4,850.77

26. Calculate reconciled checkbook balance, given the following:

Checkbook balance	$4,511.20
Interest earned	15.10
Note collected	555.10
ATM withdrawal	66.90
NSF check	12.55

26. $5,001.95

27. Calculate a reconciled balance from the following:

Checkbook balance	$2,885
Bank balance	2,999
Interest earned	22
Deposits in transit	500
Checks outstanding	620
NSF check	15
Check printing	13

27. $2,879

28. Angel's checkbook balance was $9,000. The bank statement had a balance of $10,500. Angel's bookkeeper noticed checks No. 140 for $550 and No. 145 for $205 were not yet processed by the bank. Angel made a deposit of $1,200 that had not reached the bank before preparation of the bank statement. Bank service charges totaled $40. The statement showed that the bank collected a note from Angel for $2,020 charging a $20 collection fee. Angel's bookkeeper noticed that a check for $30 was recorded as $15. What is the reconciled balance?

28. $10,945

Worked-Out Solutions to Calculations/Applications Section

22. $481.92 − $81.22 − $19.44 + $111.22 − $88.04 = $404.44

23.
```
  $ 15.88
   108.44     $463.72
 + 339.40    − 155.68 ($12.88 + $142.80)
  $463.72     $308.04
```

25. $4,800.10 − $55.32 + $105.99 = $4,850.77

26.
```
 $4,511.20
 +   15.10
 +  555.10
 −   66.90
 −   12.55
 $5,001.95
```

27.
```
 $2,885
 +   22    $2,999
 −   15    + 500
 −   13    − 620
 $2,879    $2,879
```

28.

Checkbook		Bank	
Angel's checkbook balance	$ 9,000	Bank balance	$10,500
Add:		Add:	
Collection of note (less fee)	2,000	Deposits in transit	1,200
	$11,000		$11,700
Deduct:		Deduct:	
		Outstanding checks:	
Bank service charge: $40		No. 140 $550	
Book error 15	55	No. 145 205	755
Reconciled balance	$10,945	Reconciled balance	$10,945

Word Problem Practice Quiz

Check with your instructor for complete worked-out solutions.

4–1. Jones Bank sent a bank statement to Venice Company showing an ending balance of $1,900.00. There was a service charge of $9.00 on the bank statement. The bookkeeper of Venice Company noticed in the reconciliation process a deposit in transit of $850 along with checks outstanding of $300. Complete the reconciliation for Venice assuming a beginning balance of $2,459.

4–2. Al Ring received his bank statement from Jones Bank indicating a balance of $1,751.88. Ring's checkbook showed a balance of $1,512.70. Al noticed that a check for $261.18 was outstanding. The bank statement also revealed a NSF check for $12.00 and a service charge of $10.00. Reconcile this bank statement for Al.

4–3. The Bank statement for Janet Company revealed a balance of $2,585.22, while the checkbook balance showed $2,345.84. Checks for $116.55 and $129.33 were outstanding. A check printing charge for $6.50 was on the bank statement. Prepare a bank reconciliation.

4–4. The checkbook balance of Jeep Company showed a balance of $10,636.15. The bank statement showed a balance of $9,750.44. Checks outstanding totaled $2,850.11. There was a deposit in transit of $3,525.32 along with a NSF notice for $225.00. Jeep Company had earned interest of $14.50 of its checking account. Prepare a bank reconciliation.

4–5. On May 29, 2000, Lou Co. had the following MasterCard transactions (along with some returns)—Sales: $55.10, $16.92, $101.55; Return: $6.99, $18.11. Calculate the total net deposits.

4–6. The checkbook of Moore Company showed a balance of $5,844.61. The bank statement revealed a balance of $6,950.11. Check Nos. 59 and 68 were outstanding for $750 and $219, respectively. A deposit for $435 was not listed on the bank statement. The bank collected a $600 note for Moore. Check charges for the month were $28.50. Prepare a bank reconciliation.

4–7. The checkbook balance of Roe Company is $7,069.77. The bank statement reveals a balance of $3,940.11. The bank statement showed interest earned of $24, and a service charge of $15.10. There is a deposit in transit of $6,850.44. Outstanding checks totaled $1,911.88. The bookkeeper in further analyzing the bank statement noticed a collection of a note by bank for $3,000. Roe Company forgot to deduct a check for $1,200 during the month. Prepare a bank reconciliation.

4–8. The bank statement of May 31 for Jay Company showed a balance of $6,600.11. The bookkeeper of Jay Company noticed from the bank statement that the bank had collected a note for $1,500.00. There was a deposit in transit that Jay Company made on June 1 for $5,008.10, along with the outstanding checks of $2,210.11. Check charges were $52.00. Assist the bookkeeper of Jay in preparing a reconciled statement. Assume the checkbook balance of Jay equals to $7,950.10.

4–9. On December 31, the checkbook balance of Rose Company was $8,437.00. The bank statement balance showed $9,151.88. Checks outstanding totaled $1,341.88. The statement revealed a deposit in transit of $610.55, as well as a check charge of $11.80. The company earned interest income of $7.50 that was shown on the report. The bookkeeper forgot to record a check for $12.15. Complete a bank reconciliation for Rose.

4–10. Skol's checkbook currently has a balance of $12,280.56. The bank statement shows a balance of $8,915.33. The statement revealed interest income of $27.00, along with check charges of $18.10. Skol recorded a $115 check as $100. Deposits in transit were $5,811.44. Check Nos. 85, 88, and 92 for $800.11, $700.88, and $951.32 were not returned with the statement. Prepare a bank reconciliation for Skol.

54

CHAPTER 5

Self-Paced Worksheet

Cover the answers on the right and fill in each blank. After answering the question, look to the right for your answer.

Vocabulary Review

1. A number such as 4 or -8 is called a _____.
2. An _____ is a math statement that shows equality for expressions or numbers or both.
3. A _____ is an equation that expresses in symbols a fact, rule, or principle.
4. _____ and _____ are terms of mathematical expressions.
5. The variable we are solving for is called an _____.
6. _____ are letters or symbols that represent unknowns.

1.	constant
2.	equation
3.	formula
4.	constants, variables
5.	unknown
6.	variables

Theory Tips (and/or Cautions)

7. The letter _____ could be a variable or confused with multiplication.
8. Constants have a _____ value.
9. If a variable has no number in front of it, it is assumed to be _____.
10. $A \times B$; $A \cdot B$; $A(B)$ all mean A _____ B.
11. $I = P \times R \times T$ is an example of a _____.
12. $\frac{A}{B}$ means A _____ by B.
13. $1B$ is same as _____.
14. If the equation process is addition, solve for the unknown by _____.
15. You do not _____ or divide an equation by zero.
16. When solving for an unknown that involves more than one step, do _____ and _____ before multiplication and division.
17. If an equation contains parenthesis, first multiply _____ _____ inside the parenthesis by the number or letter outside the parenthesis.

7.	X
8.	fixed
9.	one
10.	times
11.	formula
12.	divided
13.	B
14.	subtraction
15.	multiply
16.	addition; subtraction
17.	each item

Calculations/Applications

Do calculations on scrap paper as needed. Worked-out solutions are provided at end.

18. $P - \$40 = \$70$. $P =$ _____.
19. $\frac{1}{7}V = 900$. $V =$ _____.
20. $5C - C = 100$. $C =$ _____.
    $5C =$ _____.
21. $5W + 2(10 - W) = 50$. $W =$ _____.
22. Situation 5 in LU 5–2 is when total units _____ _____ _____ and know which sells better.
23. Situation 6 in LU 5–2 is when total units _____ _____ and don't know which sells best.
24. A pair of Reebok sneakers was reduced $40. The sale price was $90. The original price was _____.
25. A local KFC restaurant budgets $\frac{1}{12}$ of its monthly profits on salaries. Salaries for the month were $6,000. The monthly profit for KFC was _____.
26. Lowell Co. sold 6 times as many lamps as Ryan Co. The difference in their sales is 125. Lowell sold _____ lamps.
27. Al and Pete sold 400 homes for Century 21 Real Estate. Al sold seven times as many homes as Pete. Al sold _____ homes.

18.	$110
19.	6,300
20.	$C = 25$ $5C = 125$
21.	$W = 10$
22.	are not given
23.	are given
24.	$130
25.	$72,000
26.	150
27.	350

28. On Monday, Smith Co. sold $350 worth of calculators ($12) and watches ($10). Customers bought 5 times as many calculators as watches. How many calculators and watches did Smith sell on Monday?

28. 25 calculators; 5 watches

29. On Monday, Smith Co. sold calculators ($12) and watches ($10). A total of 30 sales of watches and calculators were $350. How many of each did Smith sell?

29. 25 calculators; 5 watches

Worked-Out Solutions to Calculations/Applications Section

18.
$$P - \$40 = \$ 70$$
$$\underline{+ 40 = + 40}$$
$$P \qquad = \$110$$

19.
$$\frac{1}{7}V = 900$$
$$7\left(\frac{1}{7}V\right) = 900\,(7)$$
$$V = 6{,}300$$

20.
$$5C - C = 100$$
$$\frac{4C}{4} = \frac{100}{4}$$
$$C = 25$$
$$5C = 125$$

21.
$$5W + 20 - 2W = 50$$
$$3W + 20 = 50$$
$$\underline{-20 = -20}$$
$$\frac{3W}{3} = \frac{30}{3}$$
$$W = 10$$

24.
$$P - \$40 = \$ 90$$
$$\underline{+ 40 \quad + 40}$$
$$P \qquad = \$130$$

25.
$$\frac{1}{12}P = \$6{,}000$$
$$12\left(\frac{1}{12}\right)P = \$6{,}000\,(12)$$
$$P = \$72{,}000$$

26.
$$6L - L = 125$$
$$\frac{5L}{5} = \frac{125}{5}$$
$$L = 25 \qquad 25 \times 6 = 150$$

27.
$$7H + H = 400$$
$$\frac{8H}{8} = \frac{400}{8}$$
$$H = 50 \qquad 7 \times 50 = 350$$

28.

Calculators	$5W$	12	$60W$
Watches	W^*	10	$+ 10W$
			$\$350$

$$60W + 10W = 350 \qquad \text{25 calculators}$$
$$\frac{70W}{70} = \frac{350}{70} \qquad \text{5 watches}$$
$$W = 5$$

For Situation 5, assign variable to one that sells the least.

29.

Calculators	C^*	12	$12C$
Watches	$30 - C$	10	$+ 10(30 - C)$
			$\$350$

$$12C + 10(30 - C) = 350$$
$$12C + 300 - 10C = 350$$
$$2C + 300 = 350$$
$$\underline{- 300 = - 300}$$
$$\frac{2C}{2} = \frac{50}{2} \qquad \text{25 calculators}$$
$$C = 25 \qquad \text{5 watches}$$
$$(30 - 25) = 5$$

For Situation 6, assign variable to most expensive.

Word Problem Practice Quiz

Check with your instructor for complete worked-out solutions.

5–1. What number decreased by 605 equals 1,090?

5–2. One eighth of all sales at Al's Diner are for cash. If cash sales for the week were $1,250, what were Al's total sales?

5–3. Christina is 9 times Judith's age. If the difference in their age is 24, how old is each?

5–4. D. Darby and J. Jonathan sell cars for Jean's Auto. Over the past year they sold 290 cars. Assume Darby sells 4 times as many cars as Jonathan. How many cars did each sell?

5–5. The Computer Store sells diskettes ($3) and boxes of computer paper ($4). If total sales were

$3,100 and customers bought 9 times as many diskettes as boxes of computer paper, what would be the number of each sold? Show proof that unit sales do equal the total dollar sales.

5–6. Pens cost $6 per carton, and rubber bands cost $4 per carton. If an order comes to a total of 70 cartons for $300, what was the specific number of cartons of pens as well as rubber bands? (Hint: Let P equal cartons of pens.)

5–7. Jim Murray and Phyllis Lowe received a total of $250,000 from a deceased relative's estate. They decided to put away $50,000 in a trust for their child and divide the remainder into $\frac{3}{4}$ for Phyllis and $\frac{1}{4}$ for Jim. How much will Phyllis and Jim receive?

5–8. In Ajax Corporation, the first shift produced $4\frac{1}{2}$ times as many lightbulbs as the second shift.

If the number of lightbulbs produced was 55,000, how many lightbulbs were produced on each shift?

5–9. Jarvis Company sells thermometers ($4) and hot water bottles ($9). If total sales were $825 and customers bought 6 times as many thermometers as hot water bottles, what would be the number of each sold? Check that your result is equal to total dollar sales.

5–10. Wrenches cost $120 per carton and hammers cost $400 per carton. An order comes in for a total of 70 cartons for $15,400. How many cartons of wrenches and hammers are involved? Check your answer. (Hint: Let H equal hammers.)

CHAPTER 6

Self-Paced Worksheet

Cover the answers on the right and fill in each blank. After answering the question, look to the right for your answer.

Vocabulary Review

1. The _____ is the beginning whole quantity to which something is being compared.
2. The _____ is a percent, decimal, or fraction that indicates the part of the base you must calculate.
3. The _____ stands for hundredths.
4. The _____ is the amount or part that results from multiplying the base times the rate.
5. The _____ _____ is the decrease in price divided by the original amount.
6. The _____ _____ is the increase in price divided by the original amount.

1. base
2. rate

3. percent
4 portion

5. percent decrease
6. percent increase

Theory Tips (and/or Cautions)

7. .008 means $\frac{8}{10}$ of _____ percent.
8. When a percent is less than 1%, the decimal conversion has at least _____ leading zeros before the whole number.
9. In rounding percents, digits to the right of the identified digit will be _____.
10. 22.5% is an example of a _____ percent.
11. In converting a mixed percent to a fraction first convert it to an _____ _____ before multiplying by 1/100.
12. The portion could be larger than the base if the rate is _____ than 100%.
13. The old year, or old price would be the _____.
14. In an increase or decrease problem, the difference in the price would be the _____.
15. The portion and rate will refer to the same part of the _____.
16. The base will be larger than the portion if the rate is _____ than 100%.
17. Portion = Base × _____.
18. The base represents _____ percent.
19. If sales are up to $4,000 a 20% increase in the new year and we are looking for sales in the old year the rate will be _____ percent of the old year.
20. The _____ is larger than the base if the rate is greater than 100%.

7. one
8. two

9. deleted
10. decimal
11. improper fraction

12. greater
13. base
14. portion
15. base
16. less
17. rate
18. 100
19. 120%

20 portion

Calculations/Applications

Do calculations on scrap paper as needed. Worked-out solutions are provided at end.

21. .006 converted to a percent is _____.
22. $7\frac{3}{4}$% converted to a decimal is _____.
23. $\frac{17}{22}$ converted to a percent is _____ (round to the nearest hundredth percent).
24. $14\frac{1}{4}$% converted to a fraction is _____.
25. 11.4% converted to a fraction is _____.
26. Twelve out of 29 students in Professor Okimato's class received an "A" grade. What percent of the class did not receive the "A" grade? (Round to the nearest tenth percent.)
27. Computer City has yet to receive 70% of his computer order. Computer City received 90 computers to date. What was the original order?
28. In 2005, a local Pizza Hut shop had sales of $450,000. In 2006, sales were up 30%. What are the shop sales in 2006?
29. The price of a Saab 9000 increased in price from $24,500 to $29,000. What was the percent increase? (Round to the nearest hundredth percent.)

21. .6%
22. .0775
23. 77.27%
24. $\frac{57}{400}$
25. $\frac{57}{500}$
26. 58.6%

27. 300 computers

28. $585,000

29. 18.37%

Worked-Out Solutions to Calculations/Applications Section

22. $7\% = .07$
$\frac{3}{4}\% = .0075$ $\Big\} = .0775$

23. $77.2727\% \rightarrow 77.27\%$
$\uparrow$

24. $14\frac{1}{4}\% = \frac{57}{4} \times \frac{1}{100} = \frac{57}{400}$

25. $11.4\% \rightarrow 11\frac{4}{10}$
$\rightarrow \frac{114}{10} \times \frac{1}{100}$
$= \frac{114}{1,000}$
$= \frac{57}{500}$

26.

12 A's 29 students	Percent did not receive A	B: 29 R: ? P: 17 (29 − 12)	$\frac{17}{29} = 58.62\%$ $= 58.6\%$

(B: 29, R: ?, P: 17)

27.

70% of order not in 90 computers received	Original order	B: ? R: .30 (100% − 70%) P: 90	$\frac{90}{.30} = 300$

(B: ?, R: .30, P: 90)

Note: 90 computers is 30% of the total, not 70%.

28.

2005 $450,000 in sales 2006 Sales up 30%	Sales of 2006	B: $450,000 R: 1.30 (100% + 30%) P: ?	$450,000 $\times$ 1.30 $585,000

(B: $450,000, R: 1.30, P: ?)

Note: The Portion is larger than the Base since Rate is greater than 100%.

29.

$24,500 old price $29,000 new price	Percent increase	B: $24,500 (orig) R: ? P: $4,500 (diff. in price)	$\frac{\$4,500}{\$24,500} = 18.367\% = 18.37\%$

(B: $24,500, R: ?, P: $4,500)

Keep in mind:
a. The Portion and Rate must relate to same piece of the Base.
b. The Portion will be larger than the Base if the Rate is greater than 100%.

Word Problem Practice Quiz

Check with your instructor for complete worked-out solutions.

6–1. A stove increased in price from $650 to $1,280. What was the percent of increase? Round to the nearest hundredth percent.

6–2. The price of a calculator dropped from $38.95 to $17.49. What was the percent decrease in price? Round to nearest tenth percent.

6–3. Joan Smith bought an IBS Personal Computer priced at $1,688. She put down 40%. What is the amount of the down payment Joan made?

6–4. Earl Miller receives an annual salary of $50,000 from PB Stationery. Today his boss informs him that he will be getting a $4,700 raise. What percent of his old salary is the $4,700 raise? Round to nearest tenth percent.

6–5. Northwest Community College has 4,900 female students. This represents 70% of the total student body. How many students attend NW Community College?

6–6. At the Museum of Fine Arts it was estimated that 40% of all visitors are from in state. On Saturday, 7,000 people attended the museum. What is the number of out-of-state people in attendance?

6–7. Sharon Fox, insurance agent, earned a commission of $840 in her first week on the job. Her commission percent is 12%. What were Sharon's total sales for the week?

6–8. John's Bookstore ordered 500 business math texts. On verifying the order, only 80 books were actually received. What percent of the order was missing?

6–9. Joshua Wright was reviewing the total accounts receivable. This month he received $180,000 from credit customers. This represented 60% of all receivables due. What is the total amount of Joshua Wright's accounts receivable?

6–10. Veek Company in 2006 had sales of $950,000. In 2007, sales were up 66%. Calculate the sales for 2007.

CHAPTER 7

Self-Paced Worksheet

Cover the answers on the right and fill in each blank. After answering the question, look to the right for your answer.

Vocabulary Review

1. A _____ _____ is the result of making an early payment within the discount period.

2. _____ _____ is the list price less the amount of trade discount.

3. _____ _____ _____ rate is found by taking the complement of each term in the discount and multiplying them together. This rate shows the actual cost to the buyer for each dollar. This rate is not rounded.

4. 1 − Net price equivalent rate equals the _____ _____ _____ rate. This rate is not rounded.

5. A _____ _____ is two or more trade discounts that are applied to the balance remaining after the previous discount is taken.

6. The amount of time to take advantage of a cash discount is the _____ _____.

7. If the discount period is missed, payment is due by the end of the _____ _____.

8. _____ _____ means seller pays cost of freight to get goods to buyer's location.

9. _____ _____ _____ means buyer pays cost of freight to getting goods to his location.

10. _____ means the same as end of month.

11. The _____ _____ is the suggested retail price paid by customers.

12. The _____ is 100% less the stated percent.

1.	cash discount
2.	net price
3.	net price equivalent
4.	single equivalent discount
5.	chain discount
6.	discount period
7.	credit period
8.	FOB destination
9.	FOB shipping point
10.	proximo
11.	list price
12.	complement

Theory Tips (and/or Cautions)

13. Trade discounts may be _____ discounts or a _____ of discounts.

14. Trade discounts are not taken on _____, returned goods, or sales tax.

15. _____ _____ are never added together.

16. The _____ _____ _____ _____ is never rounded.

17. The _____ price times the net price equivalent rate is rounded to the nearest cent.

18. The _____ _____ _____ rate shows what the buyer saves per dollar.

19. _____ _____ should be taken before cash discounts.

20. Cash discounts are taken on the _____ _____.

21. FOB destination means the _____ pays the freight cost.

22. When using the exact days in a year calendar, if the two dates are in the same year you take the _____ between the table look-up number.

23. When using the exact days in a year calendar, if the two dates are in different years from the first year table look-up will have to be _____ from 365.

24. If credit terms are 2/10 EOM and purchase is on November 5, the _____ _____ ends on December 10.

25. If credit terms are 2/10 EOM and purchase is on April 29, the discount period ends on _____.

26. Partial payments are calculated by what you can afford. The partial payment is divided by one _____ the discount rate.

13.	single; chain
14.	freight
15.	chain discounts
16.	net price equivalent rate
17.	list
18.	single equivalent discount
19.	trade discounts
20.	net price
21.	seller
22.	difference
23.	subtracted
24.	discount period
25.	June 10
26.	minus

Calculations/Applications

Do calculations on scrap paper as needed. Worked-out solutions are provided at end.

27. A chain discount of 15/3/2 results in a net price equivalent rate of _____.

27.	.80801

28. The single equivalent discount rate in #27 would be _____.
29. A cellular phone had a list price of $250 with a chain discount of 8/6. Calculate the net price and trade discount amount.

30. Complete the following:

Invoice date	Date goods received	Terms	Last day of discount period	End of credit period
a. July 8		1/10,n/30	?	?
b. March 8		2/10 EOM	?	?
c. July 9	Oct. 4	3/10,n/30 ROG	?	?
d. March 26		2/10 EOM	?	?

31. Given the following, calculate cash discount and amount paid.

   Gross amount of invoice including freight, $900
   Freight, $100
   Invoice date, 9/6
   Terms, 1/10 EOM
   Date of payment, 10/9

32. Calculate the amount to be credited and balance outstanding from the following partial payment information.

   Invoice amount, $950
   Terms, 2/10, n/60
   Invoice date, 9/20
   Partial payment date, 9/27
   Partial payment, $400

33. A Goodyear Tire Shop received an invoice showing 5 tires at $40 each, 9 tires at $70 each and 20 tires at $90 each. Shipping terms are FOB shipping point. Freight is $200. Trade discount is 10/9 and a cash discount of 2/10, N/30 is offered. Assuming Goodyear pays within the discount period, what did Goodyear pay?

28. .19199
29. $216.20 net price; $ 33.80 trade discount
30. a. July 18
   Aug. 7
   b. Apr. 10
   Apr. 30
   c. Oct. 14
   Nov. 3
   d. May 10
   May 30
31. $8.00
   $892
32. $408.16
   $541.84
33. $2,310.89

Worked-Out Solutions to Calculations/Applications Section

27.
$$\begin{array}{ccc} 100\% & 100\% & 100\% \\ -\ 15\% & -\ 3\% & -\ 2\% \\ \hline .85\ \times & .97\ \times & .98\ = .80801 \end{array}$$

28.
$$\begin{array}{c} 1.00000 \\ -\ .80801 \\ \hline .19199 \end{array}$$

29.
$$\begin{array}{cc} 100\% & 100\% \\ -\ 8\% & -\ 6\% \\ \hline .92\ \times & .94\ =\ .8648 \text{ NPER} \end{array} \qquad \begin{array}{c} 1.0000 \\ -\ .8648 \\ \hline .1352 \text{ SEDR} \end{array}$$
$$\begin{array}{cc} \times\ \$250 & \times\ \$250 \\ \hline \$216.20 & \$33.80 \end{array}$$

30. a. July 8   189
        $+\ 30$
        219 → Aug. 7

   c. Oct. 4   277
        $+\ 30$
        307 → Nov. 3

b. Cash discount ends after first 10 days of month that follows the sale. Credit period ends 20 days after discount period.

d. Cash discount ends after first 10 days of second month that follows the sale. Credit period ends 20 days after discount period.

31.
$$\begin{array}{c} \$900 \\ -\ 100 \\ \hline \$800 \times .01 = \$8.00 \\ \$800 \times .99 = \$792 + \$100 = \$892 \end{array}$$

32.
$$\frac{\$400}{1-.02} = \frac{\$400}{.98} = \$408.16 \qquad \begin{array}{c} \$950.00 \\ -\ 408.16 \\ \hline \$541.84 \end{array}$$

33.

$$5 \times \$40 = \$\ \ 200$$
$$9 \times \$70 = \ \ \ \ \ 630$$
$$20 \times \$90 = \underline{\ \ 1,800}$$
$$\$2,630 \text{ total list}$$

100%	100%
− 10%	− 9%
.90	× .91 =	.819

$$\ \ \ \ \ \ \ \ \ \ \times \ \$2,630$$
$$\ \ \ \ \ \ \ \ \ \ \$2,153.97$$

$$\$2,153.97 \times .98 = \$2,110.89$$
$$\underline{+ \ \ 200.00}$$
$$\$2,310.89$$

Word Problem Practice Quiz

Check with your instructor for complete worked-out solutions.

7-1. Alvin Corporation buys wood stoves from a wholesaler. The list price of a wood stove is $700, with a trade discount of 35%. Find the amount of trade discount and the net price of this stove.

7-2. Algene Bookstore paid a net price of $7,400 for the coming semester. The publisher offered a trade discount of 25%. What was the publisher's original list price?

7-3. Bob's Radio Shop wants to buy a line of new shortwave radios. Manufacturer A offers chain discounts of 19/10, while Manufacturer B offers terms of 18/11. Assume both manufacturers have the same list price. Which manufacturer should Bob buy from?

7-4. John's Dress Shop received an invoice dated November 8 for $1,619, with terms of 3/10, 2/15, n/60. On November 23, John's Dress Shop sent a partial payment of $715. What is the actual amount that should be credited? What is John's Dress Shop's outstanding balance?

7-5. An invoice dated 5/16/XX received by Jack's Supply indicated a balance of $7,200. This balance included a freight charge of $400. Terms of the bill were 3/10, 2/30, n/60. Assume Jack pays off the bill on May 25. What amount will he pay?

7-6. B Tool Manufacturer sold a set of jigsaws to Buy Hardware. The list price was $1,520. B Tool offered a chain discount of 4/3/2. What was the

net price of the jigsaws, and what was the total of the trade discount? Round these two answers to nearest cent.

7-7. Smith of Boston sold office equipment for $12,500 to Frank of Los Angeles. Terms of the sale are 2/10, n/30 FOB Boston. Smith has agreed to prepay the freight of $120. Assume Frank pays within the discount period. How much will they pay Smith?

7-8. A manufacturer of ice skates offered chain discounts of 6/5/1 to many of its customers. Bob's Sporting Goods ordered 30 pairs of ice skates that had a total list price of $1,800. What was the net price paid by Bob's Sporting Goods? What was the amount of the trade discount? Round answers to nearest cent.

7-9. A living room set lists for $9,000 and carries a trade discount of 30%. Freight (FOB shipping point) of $70 is not part of list price. Calculate the net price (also include cost of freight) of the living room set assuming a cash discount of 4%. What was amount of trade discount?

7-10. An invoice dated February 9 in the amount of $45,000 is received by Reliance Corporation on February 13. Cash discount terms on the invoice are 2/10, n/30. On February 18, Reliance mails a check in the amount of $9,000 as partial payment on the invoice. What is the amount of discount Reliance should receive?

CHAPTER 8

Self-Paced Worksheet
(Items with an asterisk (*) are not covered in the Brief Edition.)

Cover the answers on the right and fill in each blank. After answering the question, look to the right for your answer.

Vocabulary Review

1. The _____ _____ is the selling price less cost.
2. Gross profit minus operating expenses equals net _____.
3. The _____ is the price paid to supplier to bring merchandise into the store.
4. The original selling price less the reduction to sale price equals the _____ _____.
5. Net sales minus costs equals _____ _____.
6. Cost plus markup equals _____ _____.
7. The regular expenses of doing business are called _____ expenses.
8. Dollar markup divided by cost equals _____ _____ on _____.
9. Dollar markup divided by selling price equals _____ _____ on _____ _____.
10. The dollar markdown divided by the original selling price equals _____ _____.

1.	dollar markup
2.	income
3.	cost
4.	dollar markdown
5.	gross profit
6.	selling price
7.	operating
8.	percent markup; cost
9.	percent markup; selling price
10.	markdown percent

Theory Tips (and/or Cautions)

11. When markup is based on cost the cost is assumed to be _____ percent.
12. Selling price equals _____ plus markup.
13. The dollar markup divided by percent markup on cost equals the _____.
14. When markup is based on cost, the cost is the _____.
15. When markup is based on cost, the portion is the _____ _____.
16. When markup is based on selling price, the selling price is assumed to be _____ percent.
17. The dollar markup divided by percent markup on selling price equals the _____ _____.
18. When markup is based on selling price, the selling price is the _____.
19. When markup is based on selling price, the portion is the _____.
20. In markdowns, the dollar markdown is the _____.
21. The _____ _____ _____ in a markdown is considered to be the base.
22.* For perishables, markup is based on _____.

11.	100
12.	cost
13.	cost
14.	base
15.	selling price
16.	100
17.	selling price
18.	base
19.	cost
20.	portion
21.	original selling price
22.	cost

Calculations/Applications

Do calculations on scrap paper as needed. Worked-out solutions are provided at end.

23. Neal Wall bought a computer from A.C. Suppliers for $1,200. Neal plans to resell the computer for $1,800. What is Neal Wall's dollar markup and his percent markup on cost? Check your answer.
24. Fred Miguel bought rings for his jewelry shop that cost $90 each. Fred must mark up each ring 40% on cost. What is the dollar markup? What is the selling price of each ring? Check your answer.
25. Alice Rone sells watches. Her competitor sells a new line of watches for $30 each. Alice needs a 30% markup on cost to make her desired profit, and she must meet price competition. What cost can Alice afford to bring these watches into the store? What is the dollar markup?

23.	$600 markup; 50% markup on cost
24.	$36; $126
25.	$23.08; $6.92

26. Neal Wall bought a computer from A.C. Suppliers for $1,200. Neal plans to resell the computer for $1,800. What is Neal Wall's dollar markup and his percent markup on selling price? (Round to the nearest tenth percent.)

27. Fred Miguel bought rings for his jewelry shop that cost $90 each. Fred must mark up each ring 40% on selling price. What is the selling price of each ring? What is the dollar markup? Check your answer.

28. Alice Rone sells watches. Her competitor sells a new line of watches for $30 each. Alice needs a 30% markup on selling price to make her desired profit, and she must meet price competition. What cost can Alice afford to bring these watches into the store? What is the dollar markup?

29. Pete Burrows sells hammers for $14 that cost $8. What is Pete's percent markup at cost? (Round to the nearest tenth percent.) What is Pete's percent markup on selling price? (Round to the nearest hundredth percent.)

30. Staples bought an office desk for $400 and marked it up 30% on selling price to promote customer interest. Staples marked the desk down 5% for one week. After a week, Staples marked the desk up 2%. The last week it marked it down 8%. What is the final selling price?

31.* Joe Kiim owns a bakery. Joe baked 40 dozen bagels. Joe expects a 20% spoilage rate. The bagels cost $1.10 per dozen. Joe wants a 70% markup on cost. What should Joe charge for each dozen bagels? (Round to the nearest cent.)

26.	$600; 33.3%
27.	$150; $60
28.	$21; $9
29.	75% on cost; 42.86% on selling price
30.	$509.41
31.	$2.34 per dozen

Worked-Out Solutions to Calculations/Applications Section

23. $1,800 - $1,200 = $600 $\dfrac{\$600}{\$1,200} = 50\%$

   Check: $\dfrac{\$600}{.50} = \$1,200$

24. $S = C + M$
   $S = \$90 + .40(\$90)$ or   Check: $1.40 \times \$90 = \$126$
   $S = \$90 + \$36$
   $S = \$126$

25.* $S = C + M$
   $\$30 = C + .30C$
   $\dfrac{\$30}{1.30} = \dfrac{\cancel{1.30}C}{\cancel{1.30}}$ or $\dfrac{\$30}{1 + .30} = \dfrac{\$30}{1.30} = \$23.08$
   $\$23.08 = C$
   $\$30 - \$23.08 = \$6.92$ markup

26. $S = C + M$
   $\$1,800 = \$1,200 + M$
   $\$600 = M$
   $\dfrac{\$600}{\$1,800} = 33.3\%$

27.* $S = C + M$
   $S = \$90 + .40S$
   $\dfrac{-.40S \qquad -.40S}{\dfrac{.\cancel{60}S}{.\cancel{60}} = \dfrac{\$90}{.60}}$ or $\dfrac{\$90}{1 - .40} = \dfrac{\$90}{.60} = \$150$
   $S = \$150$
   $\$150 - \$90 = \$60$ markup

28.* $S = C + M$
   $\$30 = C + .30 (\$30)$ or $C = \$30(1 - .30)$
   $\$30 = C + \$9$ $C = \$30(.70)$
   $\dfrac{-9 \qquad -9}{\$21 = C}$ $C = \$21$
   $\$30 - \$21 = \$9$ markup

29. $\dfrac{\$14}{-\ 8}$ $\dfrac{\$6}{\$8} = 75\%$ $\dfrac{\$6}{\$14} = 42.86\%$
   $\overline{\$\ 6}$

30.*
$$S = C + M$$
$$S = \$400 + .30S$$

$$\frac{-.30S \qquad\qquad -.30S}{\frac{.70S}{.70} = \frac{\$400}{.70}} \quad \text{or} \quad \frac{\$400}{1 - .30} = \frac{\$400}{.70} = \$571.43$$

$$S = \$571.43$$

$\$571.43 \times .95 = \$542.86$

$\$542.86 \times 1.02 = \$553.71$

$\$553.71 \times .92 = \$509.41$

31.
$$TS = TC + TM$$
$$TS = \$44 + .70(\$44) \qquad \$1.10 \times 40 = \$44 \ TC$$
$$TS = \$74.80$$
$$\frac{\$74.80}{32} = \$2.34 \text{ per dozen}$$

Word Problem Practice Quiz

Check with your instructor for complete worked-out solutions.

8–1. A computer sells for $820 and is marked up 40% of the selling price. What is the cost of the computer?

8–2. Bob Hoffman sells a radio for $189.19 that cost him $91.50. What was Bob's percent of markup based on the selling price? Round to nearest percent. Check your answer. Will be slightly off due to rounding.

8–3. Reese Company buys a watch at a cost of $48.50. Reese plans to sell the watch for $79.99. What is the dollar markup as well as percent markup on cost? Round to nearest hundredth percent. Check your answer. Will be slightly off due to rounding.

8–4. Bill Spread, owner of the Bedding Shop, knows that his customers will pay no more than $300 for a comforter. Assume Bill wants a 30% markup on selling price. What is the most he could pay the manufacturer for this comforter?

8–5. John Mills sells ski gloves. He knows the most that people will pay for the gloves is $39.99. John is convinced that he needs a 28% markup based on cost. What is the most that John can pay to his supplier for gloves and still keep his selling price constant? Round to nearest cent.

8–6 Al's Department Store bought a sterling silver set for $518. Jim wants to mark up the set at 48% of the selling price. What should be the selling price of the sterling set? Round to nearest cent.

8–7. At the end of the summer, lawn mowers were advertised for 35% off regular price. John Mills saw a lawn mower with a regular price of $199. What is the dollar markdown as well as the sale price?

8–8. Mr. Fry, store manager for Vic's Appliance, is having a difficult time placing a selling price on a refrigerator that cost $899. Mr. Fry knows his boss would like to have a 35% markup based on cost. Could you help Mr. Fry with the calculation?

8–9. Angie's Bake Shop makes decorated chocolate chip cookies that cost $.30 each. Past experience shows that 20% of the cookies will crack and have to be discarded. Assume Angie wants a 65% markup based on cost and produces 400 cookies. What price should each cookie sell for? Round to nearest cent.

8–10. If, in Problem 8–9, the cracked cookies could be sold for $.20 each, what should the selling price per cookie be?

CHAPTER 9

Self-Paced Worksheet

Cover the answers on the right and fill in each blank. After answering the question, look to the right for your answer.

Vocabulary Review

1. _____ means being paid 26 times in a year.

2. The _____ _____ _____ _____ sets minimum wage standards and overtime regulations.

3. _____ _____ represents earnings before deductions.

4. A _____ _____ schedule is based on different levels of production.

5. A _____ represents an advance that will have to be repaid.

6. A _____ _____ scale uses different commission rates for different levels of net sales.

7. FICA tax requires separate reporting for _____ _____ and _____.

8. The _____ method may be used to calculate amount of federal income tax withheld.

9. _____ _____ _____ may vary from state to state.

10. A _____ _____ is a multicolumn form to record payroll.

1.	biweekly
2.	Fair Labor Standards Act
3.	gross pay
4.	differential pay
5.	draw
6.	variable commission
7.	Social Security; Medicare
8.	percentage
9.	State unemployment tax
10.	payroll register

Theory Tips (and/or Cautions)

11. A _____ is made up of thirteen weeks.

12. Biweekly period is 26 times per year, while _____ is 24 times.

13. If an overtime rate is grater than two decimal places _____ _____ round it.

14. Net pay plus _____ equals gross pay.

15. A draw is an _____ on a salesperson's commission.

16. The taxable earnings column of a _____ _____ shows the wages subject to the tax, not the actual deduction.

17. _____ has no base cut off while Social Security does.

18. The _____ pays for state and federal unemployment.

11.	quarter
12.	semimonthly
13.	do not
14.	deductions
15.	advance
16.	payroll register
17.	Medicare
18.	employer

Calculations/Applications

Do calculations on scrap paper as needed. Worked-out solutions are provided at end.

19. Calculate the total gross pay for Melvin Moore. Assume time and half for overtime. Melvin earns $8 per hour.

    Melvin's hours worked

M	T	W	Th	F	Sat
5	12	8	7	9	14

20. Based on the following schedule, what is Ron's gross pay? Ron had net sales of $180,000.

Up to $40,000	6%
$40,000–$60,000	7%
Over $60,000	$7\frac{1}{2}$%

21. Assume a 6.20% Social Security rate on $87,900 and a Medicare rate of 1.45%. What will Alice pay in, for Social Security and Medicare for this week's payroll of $1,500? To date, her cumulative earnings before this payroll were $86,700.

19.	$500
20.	$12,800
21.	SS $74.40; Med $21.75

22. From the following information, calculate Pat's weekly net pay. Use the percentage method for FIT.

Employee	Status	Claims	Gross pay	FIT	FICA SS/Med	Net pay
Pat Swan	M	2	$930			

22. FIT: $84.76;
SS: $57.66;
Med: $13.49;
Net pay: $774.09

23. Lloyd Alex has two employees who earn $500 and $800 a week. Assume a 5.4% FUTA rate. What will Lloyd pay for SUTA and FUTA for the first quarter?

23. SUTA: $729.00;
FUTA: $108.00

Worked-Out Solutions to Calculations/Applications Section

19. Total hours = 55
40 hours × $8 = $320
15 hours × $12 = 180
$500

20. ($40,000 × .06) + ($20,000 × .07) + ($120,000 × .075)
$2,400 + $1,400 + $9,000 = $12,800

21. **Social Security**   **Medicare**

$87,900 $1,500 × .0145 = $21.75
− 86,700
$ 1,200 × .062 = $74.40

22. FIT: $930.00
− 119.24 ($59.62 × 2)
$810.76
− 429.00
$381.76 = ($27.50 + .15 ($381.76))
$27.50 $57.26   = $84.76 FIT
SS: $930 × .062 = $57.66
Med: $930 × .062 = $13.49
Net pay: $930 − $84.76 − $57.66 − $13.49 = $774.09

23.   Exempt wages
13 weeks × $500 = $ 6,500   –0–
13 weeks × $800 = $10,400 $3,400
$16,900

$16,900 − $3,400 = $13,500 taxable wages

SUTA: .054 × $13,500 = $729
FUTA: .008 × $13,500 = $108

Word Problem Practice Quiz

Check with your instructor for complete worked-out solutions.

9–1. Read Jones is a salesclerk at Moe's Department Store. She is paid $7.50 per hour plus a commission of 3% on all sales. Assume Read works 35 hours and has sales of $4,800. What is her gross pay?

9–2. Staple Corporation pays its employees on a graduated commission scale: 5% on the first $40,000 sales; 6% on sales above $40,000 to $85,000; and 7% on sales greater than $85,000. Bill Burns had sales of $92,000. What commission did Bill earn?

9–3. John Hall earned $1,060 last week. He is married, paid biweekly, and claims two exemptions, What is his income tax? Use the percentage method.

9–4. Larry Johnson earns a gross salary of $3,000 each week. In week 30 what will Larry pay for Social Security and Medicare taxes?

9–5. Robyn Hartman earns $700 per week plus 5% of sales in excess of $7,000. If Robyn sells $20,000 the first week, how much are her earnings?

9–6. Joe Ross is an automobile salesman who receives a salary of $400 per week plus a commission of 6% on all sales. During a 4-week period he sold $46,900 worth of cars. What were Joe's average earnings?

9–7. B. Smith is a manager for Alve Corp. His earnings are subject to deductions for Social Security, Medicare, and FIT. B. Smith is $950 below the maximum for Social Security. What will his net pay for the week be if he earns $1,200? B. Smith is married, paid weekly, and claims three exemptions. Assume Social Security rate is 6.2% on $87,900 and Medicare is 1.45%. Use the percentage for FIT.

9–8. Al Write is a salesman who receives a $1,600 draw per week. He receives a 12% commission on all sales. Sales for Al were $192,000 for the month. What did Al receive after taking the draw into consideration? Assume a 5-week month.

9–9. Angel Frank has a cumulative earnings of $87,800 at the end of June. The first week in July she earns $1,100. What is the total amount deducted for Social Security and Medicare?

9–10. Pete Lowe, who is single and paid monthly, earns $3,300 per month. He claims a withholding allowance of one. How much FIT is deducted from his paycheck using the percentage method?

CHAPTER 10

Self-Paced Worksheet

Cover the answers on the right and fill in each blank. After answering the question, look to the right for your answer.

Vocabulary Review

1. The ordinary interest method is known as the _____ _____.

2. _____ _____ equals principal plus interest.

3. _____ _____ represents the cost of a loan.

4. The _____ _____ method is used by the Federal Reserve banks and the federal government.

5. _____ interest uses 360 days.

6. The _____ is the amount of money that is originally borrowed, loaned, or deposited.

7. The U.S. _____ allows the borrower to receive proper interest credits when paying off a loan in more than one payment before the maturity date.

8. The _____ _____ _____ is principal times rate times time.

9. _____ can be expressed as years or fractional years, used to calculate the simple interest.

10. The _____ _____ results when a partial payment is subtracted from the principal in the U.S. Rule.

Theory Tips (and/or Cautions)

11. _____ time periods can be days, months, or years.

12. Exact time can be found by the table in the *Business Math Handbook,* while _____ _____ represents 365 days.

13. Ordinary interest results in _____ interest than the exact time exact interest method.

14. _____ _____ are questioning the use of 360 days by banks.

15. In solving for the principal, given the interest, rate, and time the denominator will _____ _____ rounded.

16. When finding the time it can be converted to _____ by multiplying it by 360 or 365.

17. In the U.S. Rule, any partial payment is applied to cover the _____ due before the remainder of payment is used to lower the principal.

18. The last step of the U.S. Rule at maturity is to calculate interest from the last partial payment and _____ this interest to the adjusted balance.

19. In the U.S. Rule, the numerator of the interest calculation represents the _____ _____ _____ from previous payment date and goes to new payment date.

Calculations/Applications

Do calculations on scrap paper as needed. Worked-out solutions are provided at end.

20. Simple interest on $15,000 at $4\frac{1}{2}$% for 8 months is _____.

21. Simple interest on $20,000 at $7\frac{1}{2}$% for 17 months is _____.

22. On June 8, Reed Ching borrowed $18,000 at 7%. Reed must pay the principal and interest on September 4. Using the exact interest method, the maturity value is _____.

23. The maturity value in #22 would be _____ using the ordinary interest method.

---

1. Banker's Rule
2. maturity value
3. simple interest
4. exact interest

5. ordinary
6. principal
7. Rule

8. simple interest formula

9. time

10. adjusted balance

11. loan
12. exact interest

13. higher
14. consumer groups
15. not be

16. days
17. interest

18. add

19. number of days

20. $450
21. $2,125
22. $18,303.78

23. $18,308

70

24. Complete the following (assume 360 days).

	Principal	Rate	Time	Simple interest
a.	?	6%	90 days	$18,000
b.	$6,000	?	300 days	$400
c.	$2,500	$7\frac{1}{2}$%	?	$550

25. Aray Foger borrowed $7,000 for 60 days at 7%. On day 20, Aray made a $800 partial payment. On day 45, Aray made a $1,200 partial payment. What is Aray's ending balance under the U.S. Rule?

24. a. $1,200,000;
    b. 8%;
    c. 1,056 days

25. $5,072.24

Worked-Out Solutions to Calculations/Applications Section

20. $15,000 \times .045 \times \frac{8}{12} = $450

21. $20,000 \times .075 \times \frac{17}{12} = $2,125

22. Sept 4 → 247
    June 8 → $\underline{159}$
    $ 88$ $\quad$ $18,000 \times .07 \times \frac{88}{365} = $303.78
    $MV = $18,000 + $303.78 = $18,303.78$

23. $18,000 \times .07 \times \frac{88}{360} = $308
    $MV = $18,000 + $308 = $18,308$

24. a. $\dfrac{\$18,000}{.06 \times \dfrac{90}{360}} = $1,200,000

    b. $\dfrac{\$400}{\$6,000 \times \dfrac{300}{360}} = .08 = 8\%$

    c. $\dfrac{\$550}{\$2,500 \times .075} = 2.9\overline{3} \times 360 = 1,056$ days

25. $7,000 \times .07 \times \frac{20}{360} = $27.22

    $$\begin{array}{r} \$800.00 \\ -\ 27.22 \\ \hline \$772.78 \end{array}$$

    $$\begin{array}{r} \$7,000.00 \\ -\ 772.78 \\ \hline \end{array}$$
    $6,227.22 \times .07 \times \frac{25}{360} = $30.27

    $$\begin{array}{r} \$1,200.00 \\ -\ 30.27 \\ \hline \$1,169.73 \end{array}$$

    $$\begin{array}{r} \$6,227.22 \\ -1,169.73 \\ \hline \end{array}$$
    $5,057.49 \times .07 \times \frac{15}{360} = $14.75

    Balance owed $5,072.24 ($14.75 + $5,057.49)

Word Problem Practice Quiz

Check with your instructor for complete worked-out solutions.

10–1. Abby Ellen took out a loan of $45,000 to pay for her child's education. The loan would be repaid at the end of 8 years in one payment with $12\frac{1}{2}$% interest. How much interest is due? What is the total amount Abby has to pay at the end of the loan?

10–2. Jill Ring took out a simple interest loan for $20,000 at $6\frac{1}{2}$% for 19 months. What is the total interest cost (to nearest cent) for Jill?

10–3. Jennifer Rick went to Sunshine Bank to borrow $3,500 at a rate of $10\frac{3}{4}$%. The date of the loan was September 7. Jennifer hoped to repay the loan on January 15. Assume the loan is ordinary interest. What will be the interest cost on

January 15? How much will Jennifer totally repay?

10–4. Jill Blum has a talk with Jennifer Rick (Problem 10–3) and suggests she consider the loan on exact interest. Recalculate the loan for Jennifer under this assumption.

10–5. Bob Lopes visited his local bank to see how long it will take for $1,000 to amount to $1,900 at a simple interest rate of 10%. Can you solve Bob's problem?

10–6. Margie Jones owns her own car. Her November monthly interest was $205. The rate is $13\frac{1}{2}$%. Find out what Margie's principal balance is at the beginning of November. Use 360 days. (In calculation, do not round denominator answer before dividing into numerator.)

10–7. Jane took out a loan for $16,800 at $9\frac{3}{4}$% on April 2, 2005. The loan is due January 8, 2006. Using exact time, ordinary interest, what is the interest cost? What total amount will Jane pay on January 8, 2006?

10–8. Terry Ball took out the same loan as Jane (Problem 10–7), but his terms were exact interest. What is Terry's difference in interest? What will Terry pay on January 8, 2006?

10–9. Bill Brody borrowed $12,500 on an 11% 120-day note. After 65 days, Bill paid $500 toward the note. On day 89, Bill paid an additional $4,500. What is the final balance due? Work out the total interest and ending balance due by the U.S. Rule.

CHAPTER 11

Self-Paced Worksheet

Cover the answers on the right and fill in each blank. After answering the question, look to the right for your answer.

Vocabulary Review

1. For a simple discount note the interest banks deduct in advance is the _____ _____.

2. Principal plus interest equals _____ _____.
3. The _____ _____ is also the principal of the note.
4. The company extending credit of an interest-bearing note is called the _____.
5. The company issuing the note and borrowing the money is called the _____.
6. A _____ note states that the borrower will repay a certain sum at a fixed time in the future.
7. The _____ of the note represents what one receives after deducting the bank discount from the maturity value of a note.
8. The _____ _____ is the true rate of interest.
9. A _____ _____ represents a loan to the federal government.
10. A _____ _____ _____ provides immediate financing up to an approved limit.

1. bank discount

2. maturity value
3. face value
4. payee
5. maker
6. promissory

7. proceeds

8. effective rate
9. Treasury bill
10. line of credit

Theory Tips (and/or Cautions)

11. The _____ _____ of the a non-interest-bearing note is the same as its face value.
12. A promissory note for a loan is usually _____ than one year.
13. The _____ _____ is higher for a simple discount note, since interest is deducted in advance.
14. The purchase price (or proceeds) of a Treasury bill is the value of the Treasury bill _____ the discount.
15. In the discounting process, the discount period represents the number of days the _____ will have to wait for the note to come due.
16. Instead of discounting notes, many companies set up _____ _____ _____ so that additional financing is immediately available.
17. A _____ _____ can be interest-bearing or noninterest-bearing.
18. In discounting an interest-bearing note before maturity, the first step is to calculate the _____ _____.
19. To calculate the _____ _____ you must use the maturity value times the bank discount rate times the number of days the bank waits for the note to come due divided by 360.

11. maturity value
12. less
13. effective rate

14. less

15. bank

16. lines of credit

17. promissory note
18. maturity value

19. bank discount

Calculations/Applications

Do calculations on scrap paper as needed. Worked-out solutions are provided at end.

20. Andre Fox borrowed $15,000 on a noninterest-bearing, simple discount, $7\frac{1}{2}$%, 90-day note. Assume ordinary interest. What is (a) maturity value, (b) the bank's discount, (c) Andre's proceeds, and (d) the effective rate to nearest hundredth percent?

21. Joy Lindman buys a $10,000 13-week Treasury bill at $8\frac{1}{4}$%. What is her effective rate? Round to the nearest hundredth percent.

22. Frost Corporation accepted a $20,000, 8%, 90-day note on July 8. Frost discounts the note on September 6 at East Bank at 9%. What proceeds did Frost receive?

20. **a.** $15,000;
    b. $281.25;
    c. $14,718.75;
    d. 7.64%;

21. 8.42%

22. $20,247

Worked-Out Solutions to Calculations/Applications Section

20. b. $\$15{,}000 \times .075 \times \dfrac{90}{360} = \$281.25$

  c. $\$15{,}000 - \$281.25 = \$14{,}718.75$

  d. $\dfrac{\$281.25}{\$14{,}718.75 \times \dfrac{90}{360}} = 7.64\%$

21. $\$10{,}000 \times .0825 \times \dfrac{13}{52} = \$206.25$

  $\$10{,}000 - \$206.25 = \$9{,}793.75$

  $\dfrac{\$206.25}{\$9{,}793.75 \times \dfrac{13}{52}} = 8.42\%$

22. Interest $= \$20{,}000 \times .08 \times \dfrac{90}{360} = \$400$

  1. $MV = \$20{,}000 + \$400 = \$20{,}400$

  2. Sept. 6 $\rightarrow$ 249
  July 8 $\rightarrow$ 189
  $\overline{60}$ $90 - 60 = 30$ days

  3. Bank discount $= \$20{,}400 \times .09 \times \dfrac{30}{360} = \$153$

  4. Proceeds $= \$20{,}400 - \$153 = \$20{,}247$

Word Problem Practice Quiz

Check with your instructor for complete worked-out solutions.

Use ordinary interest in your calculations.

11–1. James Bank discounts an 89-day note for $15,000 at 12%. Find the bank discount and proceeds.

11–2. In Problem 11–1, what is the effective rate of interest when the bank discounts the note at 12%? Round to nearest hundredth percent.

11–3. Jarvis Corporation accepted an $18,000 note on August 12. Terms of the note were $12\frac{3}{4}\%$ for 90 days. Jarvis discounted the note on September 20 at Shaw Bank at 13%. What net proceeds did Jarvis receive?

11–4. Michele Fross borrowed $6,000 for 120 days from Jones Bank. The bank discounted the note at 9%. What proceeds does Michele receive? Calculate effective interest rate to nearest hundredth percent.

11–5. On November 30, Smith Company accepted a 120-day, $15,000 noninterest-bearing note from B Manufacturer. What is the maturity value of the note?

11–6. On July 12 at the Sunshine Bank, Joyce Corporation discounted a $5,000, 90-day note dated June 20. Sunshine's discount rate was $11\frac{3}{4}\%$. How much did Joyce Corporation receive? Assume $5,000 is the maturity value.

11–7. Roger Corporation accepted an $8,000, 11%, 120-day note dated August 8 from June Company in settlement of a past bill. On October 25, Roger Corporation discounted the note at the bank at 12%. What is the note's maturity value, discount period, and bank discount? What are the net proceeds to Roger Corporation?

11–8. On April 12, Dr. Brown accepted a $10,000, 10%, 60-day note from Bill Moss granting a time extension on a past-due account. Dr. Brown discounted the note at the bank at 12% on May 20. What proceeds does Dr. Brown receive?

11–9. On May 5, Scott Rinse accepted a $12,000 note in granting a time extension of a bill for goods bought by Ron Prentice. Terms of the note were 13% for 90 days. On July 2, Scott could no longer wait for the money and discounted the note at Able Bank at 11%. What are Scott's proceeds?

11–10. Jensen Furniture wants to buy a $5,000 computer with a huge $1,000 cash discount. Jensen needs more cash to pay the bill. It is considering discounting a 120-day note dated May 12 with a maturity value of $5,000. Hunt Bank has a discount rate of 15% on May 18. Should Jensen discount the note?

CHAPTER 12

Self-Paced Worksheet

Cover the answers on the right and fill in each blank. After answering the question, look to the right for your answer.

Vocabulary Review

1. _____ is calculating the interest periodically over the life of the loan and adding it to the principal.

2. _____ _____ looks at how much money will have to be deposited today (or at some date) to reach a specific amount at maturity (in the future).

3. _____ are calculated by the number of years times the number of times compounded per year.

4. The _____ can be found by the annual rate divided by the number of times compounded per year.

5. Compounded _____ means the interest is calculated on the balance every six months.

6. The _____ _____ (APY) is calculated by the interest for 1 year divided by the principal.

7. The stated or _____ rate is one which the bank calculates interest.

Theory Tips (and/or Cautions)

8. To see how long to double a sum of money at different interest rates with annual compounding, divide 72 by the _____ _____.

9. Compounding goes from the present value to the _____ _____.

10. Present value goes from the future value to the _____ _____.

11. Compounded _____ means interest is calculated on the balance every 3 months.

12. Compound amounts less the principal equals _____ _____.

13. Compounding results in _____ interest than simple interest.

14. In the calculation of effective rate, the portion is the _____ for one year.

15. The APY or effective rate for $1 can be seen in the _____ table.

16. The table factors in the _____ _____ table are larger than 1.

17. The table factors in the _____ _____ table are less than 1.

18. A present value answer can be checked by using the _____ _____ table.

Calculations/Applications

Do calculations on scrap paper as needed. Worked-out solutions are provided at end.

19. Alfred Rodriguez deposits $8,000 in Yoma Bank which pays 6% interest compounded quarterly. How much will Alfred have in his account at the end of 6 years?

20. Give the following, calculate the effective rate (to the nearest hundredth percent): Principal, $9,000; Interest rate, 8% compounded semiannually.

21. $1,800 compounded daily for 10 years will grow to _____ at 6.50%.

22. Jim Henson wants to buy his son a Toyota Land Cruiser in 5 years. The cost of the car should be $40,000. Assuming a bank rate of 6% compounded quarterly, how much must Jim put in the bank today?

23. Check your answer in #22 by the compound table.

Answers column:

1. compounding
2. present value
3. periods
4. rate
5. semiannually
6. effective rate
7. nominal
8. interest rate
9. future value
10. present value
11. quarterly
12. compound interest
13. higher
14. interest
15. compound
16. compound interest
17. present value
18. compound value
19. $11,436
20. 8.16%
21. $3,447.72
22. $29,700
23. $40,002

Worked-Out Solutions to Calculations/Applications Section

19. $\frac{6\%}{4} = 1.5\%$ 6 yrs. × 4 = 24 periods

    $8,000 × 1.4295 = $11,436

20. 4%, 2 periods (2 × 1)

    $9,000 × 1.0816 = $9,734.40
                      − 9,000.00
                      $ 734.40

    $\frac{\$734.40}{\$9,000} = 8.16\%$

21. $1,800 \times 1.9154 = \$3,447.72$

22. $\dfrac{6\%}{4} = 1\dfrac{1}{2}\%$ 5 yrs. $\times$ 4 = 20 periods

$40,000 \times .7425 = \$29,700$

23. $1\dfrac{1}{2}\%$, 20 periods   1.3469

$29,700 \times 1.3469 = \$40,002$ off slightly due to rounding of table factors.

Word Problem Practice Quiz

Check with your instructor for complete worked-out solutions.

12–1. Al Baker deposited $30,000 into Victory Bank which pays 12% interest compounded semiannually. How much will Al have in his account at the end of 4 years?

12–2. Ann Kate, owner of Ann's Sport Shop, loaned $13,000 to Rusty Katz to help him open an art shop. Rusty pans to repay Ann at the end of 5 years with 6% interest compounded quarterly. How much will Ann receive at the end of 5 years?

12–3. Jill Fonda opened a new savings account. She deposited $18,000 at 12% interest compounded semiannually. At the beginning of the year 4, Jill deposits an additional $50,000 that is also compounded semiannually at 12%. At the end of 6 years, what is the balance in Jill's account?

12–4. Rochelle Kotter wants to attend S.M.V. University. She will need $55,000 4 years from today. Her bank pays 12% interest compounded semiannually. What amount must Rochelle deposit today so she will have $55,000 in 4 years?

12–5. Margaret Foster wants to buy a new camper in 7 years. Margaret estimates the cost of the camper will be $7,200. If she invests $4,000 now, at a rate of 12% interest compounded semiannually, will she have enough money to buy her camper at the end of 7 years?

12–6. Karen is having difficulty deciding whether to put her savings in Mystic Bank or in Four Rivers Bank. Mystic offers a 10% interest rate compounded semiannually, while Four Rivers offers 12% interest compounded annually. Karen has $30,000 to deposit and expects to withdraw the money at the end of 5 years. Which bank gives Karen the best deal?

12–7. Steven deposited $15,000 at York Bank at 10% interest compounded semiannually. What was the effective rate? Round to nearest hundredth percent.

12–8. Al Miller, owner of Al's Garage, estimates that he will need $25,000 for new equipment in 20 years. Al decided to put aside the money today so it will be available in 20 years. His bank offers him 8% interest compounded semiannually. How much must Al invest today to have $25,000 in 20 years?

12–9. Ray Long wants to retire in Arizona when he is 70 years of age. He is now 55 and believes he will need $200,000 to retire comfortably. To date, Ray has set aside no retirement money. Assume Ray gets 12% interest compounded semiannually. How much must be invest today to meet his goal of $200,000?

12–10. Kevin Moore deposited $12,000 in a new savings account at 6% interest compounded quarterly. At the beginning of year 4, Kevin deposits an additional $40,000 also compounded quarterly at 6%. At the end of 6 years, what is the balance in Kevin's account?

CHAPTER 13

Self-Paced Worksheet

Cover the answers on the right and fill in each blank. After answering the question, look to the right for the answer.

Vocabulary Review

1. An _____ is a stream of equal payments made at periodic times.

2. An _____ _____ is an annuity that is paid (or received) at the end of the time period.

3. An _____ _____ is an annuity that is paid (or received) at the beginning of the time period.

4. Annuities that have stated beginning and ending dates are called _____ _____.

5. Beginning and ending dates of _____ _____ are uncertain (not fixed).

6. A _____ _____ is an annuity in which the stream of deposits with appropriate interest will equal a specified amount in the future.

7. The _____ _____ _____ _____ is the amount of money needed today to receive a specified steam (annuity) of money in the future.

1.	annuity
2.	ordinary annuity
3.	annuity due
4.	annuities certain
5.	contingent annuities
6.	sinking fund
7.	present value of annuity

Theory Tips (and/or Cautions)

8. The value of an annuity is the value of a series of payments _____ interest.

9. With an ordinary annuity, regular payments (or deposits) are made at the _____ of the period.

10. With an annuity due, regular payments (or deposits) are made at the _____ of the period.

11. What we call _____ _____ in compounding is now called the value of annuity.

12. Ordinary annuities and annuities due both find _____ _____.

13. The _____ _____ will give a higher final value than _____ _____ since money is put in at the beginning of the period.

14. The _____ _____ of an ordinary annuity finds the present worth.

15. In calculating annuity due by the ordinary annuity table, you should add _____ period and subtract _____ payment.

16. Annuity payments do not have to be _____.

17. The sinking fund payment can be checked by the _____ _____ table.

18. In a sinking fund you determine the amount of _____ _____ you need to achieve a financial goal.

8.	plus
9.	end
10.	beginning
11.	maturity value
12.	future value
13.	annuity due; ordinary annuity
14.	present value
15.	one; one
16.	yearly
17.	ordinary annuity
18.	periodic payment

Calculations/Applications

Do calculations on scrap paper as needed. Worked-out solutions are provided at end.

19. Calculate by table the value of an investment after 3 years on an ordinary annuity of $6,000 made semiannually at 6%.

20. Redo your calculation in #19 assuming an annuity due.

21. Nancy Cram won the Boston Lottery and will receive a $5,000 check at the beginning of each 6 months for the next 7 years. If Nancy deposits each check into an account that pays 8%, how much will she have at the end of the 7 years?

22. What must you invest today to receive a $6,000 annuity for 10 years quarterly at 8% annual rate? All withdrawals will be made at the end of each period.

23. Pete O'Sullivan wants to set up a scholarship fund to provide 6 $4,000 scholarships for the next 5 years. If money can be invested at an annual rate of 6%, how much should Pete invest today?

19.	$38,810.40
20.	$39,975
21.	$95,118
22.	$164,132.40
23.	$101,097.60

24. Long Co. issued bonds that will mature to a value of $80,000 in 8 years. Long is setting up a sinking fund. Interest rates are 8% compounded quarterly. What will be the amount of each sinking fund payment? Verify your answer by the amount of annuity. It will be off due to rounding of tables. (Use tables in *Business Math Handbook*.)

24. $1,808

Worked-Out Solutions to Calculations/Applications Section

19. $\frac{6\%}{2} = 3\%$ 3 yrs. × 2 = 6 periods

$6,000 × 6.4684 = $38,810.40

20. 3%, 7 periods
$6,000 × 7.6625 = $45,975
$\underline{\hspace{1.2em}- 6,000}$
$39,975

21. $\frac{8\%}{2} = 4\%$ 7 yrs. × 2 = 14
$\underline{\hspace{2.5em}+ 1}$
15 periods

$5,000 × 20.0236 = $100,118
$\underline{\hspace{1.2em}- 5,000}$
$ 95,118

22. $\frac{8\%}{4} = 2\%$ 10 yrs. × 4 = 40 periods

$6,000 × 27.3554 = $164,132.40

23. 6%, 5 periods
$24,000 × 4.2124 = $101,097.60

24. $\frac{8\%}{4} = 2\%$ 8 yrs. × 4 = 32 periods

$80,000 × .0226 = $1,808
Verify: $1,808 × 44.2269 = $79,962 (due to rounding of tables)

Word Problem Practice Quiz

Check with your instructor for complete worked-out solutions.

13–1. Charlie Gold made deposits of $700 at end of each year for 7 years. The interest rate is 7% compounded annually. What is the value of Charlie's annuity at end of 7 years?

13–2. James Will promised to pay his son $500 semiannually for 5 years. Assume James can invest his money at 8% in an ordinary annuity. How much must James invest today to pay his son $500 semiannually for 5 years?

13–3. Bill Martin invests $6,000 at the end of each year for 7 years in an ordinary annuity at 6% interest compounded annually. What is the final value of Bill's investment at the end of year 7?

13–4. Alice Long has decided to invest $400 semiannually for 5 years in an ordinary annuity at 10%. As her financial advisor, could you calculate for Alice the total cash value of the annuity at the end of year 5?

13–5. At the beginning of each period for 5 years, Rob Flynn invests $800 semiannually at 12%. What is the cash value of this annuity due at the end of year 5?

13–6. Murphy Company borrowed money that must be repaid in 5 years. So that the loan will be repaid at end of year 5, the company invests $8,500 at end of each year at 8% interest compounded annually. What was the amount of the original loan?

13–7. Jane Frost wants to receive semiannual payments of $25,000 for 10 years. How much must she deposit at her bank today at a 10% interest rate compounded semiannually?

13–8. Jeff Associates borrowed $70,000. The company plans to set up a sinking fund that will repay the loan at the end of 20 years. Assume a 12% interest rate compounded semiannually. What must Jeff pay into the fund each period? Check your answer by table.

13–9. At the beginning of each period for 7 years, Michael Ring invested $1,200 at 10% interest compounded semiannually. What is the value of this annuity due?

13–10. Jim Green wants to receive $8,000 each year for the next 12 years. Assume an interest rate of 6% compounded annually. How much must Jim invest today?

CHAPTER 14

Self-Paced Worksheet

Cover the answers on the right and fill in each blank. After answering the question, look to the right for your answer.

Vocabulary Review

1. _____ is the process of paying back a loan (principal and interest) by equal periodic payments.
2. Cash price less down payment equals _____ _____.
3. The _____ _____ _____ is the true or effective annual interest rate charged by sellers.
4. The sum of daily balances divided by the number of days in the billing cycle equals the _____ _____ _____.
5. A _____ _____ results when money is borrowed by the holder of a credit card.
6. The total of all payments less actual loan cost equals the _____ _____.
7. The deferred payment price is the total of all monthly payments _____ down payment.
8. Open-end credit is a _____ credit account.
9. The Rule of 78 is one method to compute _____ on consumer finance loans.
10. The _____ is the finance charge a customer receives for paying off a loan early.

1.	amortization
2.	amount financed
3.	annual percentage rate
4.	average daily balance
5.	cash advance
6.	finance charge
7.	plus
8.	revolving
9.	rebates
10.	rebate

Theory Tips (and/or Cautions)

11. The finance charge can include the cost of _____ reports, mandatory bank fees, etc.
12. APR can be calculated by using _____.
13. The Truth in Lending Act doesn't dictate what can be _____ for interest.
14. The loan amortization table is per _____. The table is used to calculate the monthly payment.
15. The U.S. Rule applied partial payment to interest _____ and then the remainder of the payment _____ the principal.
16. In calculating the rebate fraction, the _____ represents the sum of digits based on the number of months to go.
17. The denominator of the rebate fraction represents the sum of digits based on the _____ number of months of the loan.
18. Most companies calculate the _____ _____ as a percentage of the average daily balance.
19. A cash advance is a _____ _____ from a credit card company.
20. In calculating the average daily balance, the days of the _____ _____ has to be known to arrive at the final number of days of the current balance.

11.	credit
12.	tables
13.	charged
14.	$1,000
15.	first; reduces
16.	numerator
17.	total
18.	finance charge
19.	cash loan
20.	billing cycle

Calculations/Applications

Do calculations on scrap paper as needed. Worked-out solutions are at the end.

21. Gail Sentner bought a new Chevrolet for $16,500, putting down $500 and paying $300 per month for 60 months. Calculate:

   a. Amount financed.
   b. Finance charge.
   c. Deferred payment price.
   d. APR by table. (Use tables in *Business Math Handbook*.)
   e. Monthly payment by formula.

22. Dan Carl is buying a new Welbilt boat for $9,500. Dan puts down $2,000 and is financing the balance at 11% for 60 months. What is his monthly payment (use the loan amortization table)?

21.	**a.** $16,000
	b. $2,000
	c. $18,500
	d. 4.5%–4.75%
	e. $300
22.	$163.05

23. From the following, calculate the finance charge rebate and final payoff:

Loan for 12 months; $6,200; end-of-month loan is repaid: 8; monthly payment; $575

24. Paula Franc bought a desk for $900. She pays $100 a month and is charged $3\frac{1}{2}\%$ interest on the unpaid balance. What is Paula's balance outstanding at the end of month 1?

25. Calculate the average daily balance and finance charge from the following (30-day billing cycle):

7/21	Billing date	Previous balance	$400
7/28	Payment		$ 40 credit
7/31	Charge		$ 60
8/6	Payment		$ 10 credit
8/13	Cash advance		$ 50

Finance charge is $1\frac{1}{2}\%$ on average daily balance.

23. $89.74; $2,210.26

24. $831.50

25. $416.33; $6.24

Worked-Out Solutions for Calculations/Applications Section

21. **a.** $16,500 − $500 = $16,000

  b. $18,000 (60 × $300) − $16,000 = $2,000

  c. $18,000 (60 × $300) + $500 = $18,500

  d. $\dfrac{\$2,000}{\$16,000} \times \$100 = \$12.5$ between 4.5% and 4.75%

  e. $\dfrac{\$2,000 + \$16,000}{60} = \$300$

22. $\dfrac{\$7,500}{\$1,000} = 7.5 \times \$21.74 = \$163.05$

23. **Step 1:**
$$\begin{array}{r} 12 \times \$575 = \$6,900 \\ 8 \times \$575 = \underline{4,600} \\ \$2,300 \end{array}$$

  Step 2:
$$\begin{array}{r} 12 \times \$575 = \$6,900 \\ \underline{-6,200} \\ \$\ 700 \end{array}$$

  Step 3: 12 − 8 = 4

  Step 4: $\dfrac{10}{78}$

  Step 5: $\dfrac{10}{78} \times \$700 = \$89.74$

  Step 6: $2,300 − $89.74 = $2,210.26

24. $900 × 3.5% = $31.50

  $100 − $31.50 = $68.50

  $900 − $68.50 = $831.50

25.
7 × $400	$ 2,800
3 × $360	1,080
6 × $420	2,520
7 × $410	2,870
7 × $460	3,220
(30 − 23)	$12,490

$\dfrac{\$12,490}{30} = \$416.33$

FC = $416.33 × .015 = $6.24

Word Problem Practice Quiz

Check with your instructor for complete worked-out solutions.

14–1. Andy Troll bought a new delivery truck for $16,000. Andy put a down payment of $3,000 and paid $255 monthly for 60 months. What is the total amount financed and the total finance charge that Andy paid at the end of the 60 months?

14–2. Joan Porl read the following advertisement: Price, $17,000; down payment, $500 cash or trade; amount financed, $16,500; $399 per month for 60 months; finance charge, $7,440; and total payments $23,940.
(1) Check finance charge and (2) calculate the APR by table.

14–3. Barry Crate bought a desk for $7,000. Based on his income, he could only afford to pay back $900 per month. There is a charge of $2\frac{1}{2}\%$ interest on the unpaid balance. The U.S. Rule is used in the calculation. Could you calculate at the end of month 2 the balance outstanding?

14–4. Tony Jean borrowed $8,150 to travel to Europe to see his son Bill. His loan was to be paid in 48 monthly installments of $198. At the end of 11 months, Tony's daughter Joan convinced him that he should pay off the loan early. What is Tony's rebate and his payoff amount?

14–5. Jim Smith bought a new boat for $9,000. Jim put down $1,000 and financed the balance at 11% for 60 months. What is his monthly payment? Use the Loan Amortization table.

14–6. Al Rolf bought an air conditioner with $150 down and 38 equal monthly installments of $35. The total purchase price (cash price) of the air conditioner was $1,050. Al decided to pay off the bill after the 30th payment. What is Al entitled to as a rebate on the finance charge? What will Al's payoff be?

14–7. Joanne Flynn bought a new boat for $15,000. She put a $2,000 down payment on the boat. The bank's loan was for 48 months. Finance charges totaled $4,499.84. Assume Joanne decides to pay off the loan at the end of the 26th month. What rebate would she be entitled to and what is the actual payoff amount? Round monthly payment to nearest cent.

14–8. Calculate APR by table for the following advertisement:
$98.50 per month; cash price, $2,899; down payment $199, cash or trade; 36 months with bank approved credit, amount financed, $2,700; finance charge, $846; total payments, $3,546.

14–9. From the following facts, Bill Jess has requested you to calculate the average daily balance and finance charge.

30-day billing cycle			
3/18	Billing date	Previous balance	$880
3/24	Payment		70
3/29	Charge		350
4/5	Payment		30
4/9	Charge		400

Finance charge is 1% of average daily balance.

14–10. Glen James borrowed $7,200 from Able Loan Company. The loan is to be repaid in 48 monthly installments of $199. At the end of 14 months, Glen decided to pay off the loan. What is Glen's rebate and payoff amount?

81

CHAPTER 15

Self-Paced Worksheet

Cover the answers on the right and fill in each blank. After answering the question, look to the right for your answer.

Vocabulary Review

1. The rate for an _____ _____ mortgage is lower than a fixed rate mortgage.
2. The _____ _____ shows how each monthly payment is broken down into interest and principal reduction.
3. A _____ mortgage is paid every two weeks rather than monthly.
4. A _____ _____ loan provides a cheap and readily accessible line of credit backed by equity in your home.
5. A _____ is a one-time payment made at closing.
6. A _____ is the cost of home less the down payment.
7. A special account set up to protect the bank is called an _____ account.
8. In a _____ _____ mortgage, the borrower pays less at the beginning of the mortgage. As years go on, the payment increases.
9. When property passes from the seller to the buyer, _____ _____ may include credit reports, recording costs, lawyer's fees, points, title search, etc.

1. adjustable rate
2. amortization schedule
3. biweekly
4. home equity

5. point
6. mortgage
7. escrow
8. graduated payment

9. closing costs

Theory Tips (and/or Cautions)

10. In a 30-year fixed mortgage, you are locked in to the interest rate, unless you _____ to get a lower interest rate.
11. In a 15-year fixed rate mortgage you need a larger down payment. The monthly payment will be _____.
12. A graduated-payment may have _____ APR than fixed or variable rates.
13. The _____ _____ requires 26 biweekly payments a year. It shortens the term loan and saves a substantial amount of interest.
14. Home equity loans are _____ deductible.
15. Points are a _____ charge that is a percent of the mortgage.
16. A rise in _____ rates could cost a home buyer thousands of extra dollars in interest cost over the life of a mortgage.
17. In the early payments of a mortgage, most of the monthly payment goes to cover _____ with a smaller reduction in _____.
18. If you plan to own your home for a short time _____ may not be an attractive alternative to get a lower rate of interest.

10. refinance

11. higher

12. higher
13. biweekly mortgage

14. tax
15. one-time
16. interest

17. interest; principal

18. refinancing

Calculations/Applications

Do calculations on scrap paper as needed. Worked-out solutions are provided at end.

19. Twila Griffen bought a new condominium for $110,000. She put down 10% and obtained a mortgage at 8% for 25 years. What is her (a) monthly payment, (b) the total interest cost, and (c) cost of interest for the first payment?
20. Alison Wolfe bought a new chalet for $80,000 at 9% for 30 years. Prepare an amortization schedule for the first two periods.

21. Aster Smith bought a home in Ventura, California for $110,000. He put down 20% and obtained a mortgage for 30 years at 10%. (a) What is Aster's monthly payment? (b) What is the total interest cost of the loan?
22. If in Problem #21 the rate of interest is 12%, what is the difference in interest cost?

19. a. $764.28
    b. $130,284
    c. $660
20. 1. $600, $44
       $79,956
    2. $599.67, $44.33
       $79,911.67

21. a. $772.64
    b. $190,150.40

22. $47,836.80

19. $\dfrac{\$99,000}{\$1,000} = 99 \times \$7.72 = \$764.28$

    $300 \times \$764.28 = \$229,284$
    $\underline{-\ 99,000}$
    $\$130,284$

    $\$99,000 \times .08 \times \dfrac{1}{12} = \$660$

Note:

   12×25 years $= 300$ payments

20. $\dfrac{\$80,000}{\$1,000} = 80 \times \$8.05 = \$644$

Payment	Principal	Interest	Principal reduction	Balance of principal
1	\$80,000	\$600 $\left(\$80,000 \times .09 \times \dfrac{1}{12}\right)$	\$44	\$79,956
2	\$79,956	\$599.67 $\left(\$79,956 \times .09 \times \dfrac{1}{12}\right)$	\$44.33	\$79,911.67

21. $\dfrac{\$88,000}{\$1,000} = 88 \times \$8.78 = \$772.64$

    $360 \times \$772.64 = \$278,150.40$
    $\underline{-\ 88,000.00}$
    $\$190,150.40$

22. $88 \times \$10.29\ \ =\ \$905.52$
   $360 \times \$905.52 = 325,987.20$
   $\underline{-\ 88,000.00}$
   $237,987.20$
   $\underline{-190,150.40}$
   $\$47,836.80$

Word Problem Practice Quiz

Check with your instructor for complete worked-out solutions.

15–1. Jeff Jones purchased a new condominium for $129,000. The bank required a $30,000 down payment. Assume a rate of 10% on a 25-year mortgage. What is Jeff's monthly payment and total interest cost?

15–2. Bill Allen bought a home in Arlington, Texas, for $118,000. He put down 30% and obtained a mortgage for 30 years at 11%. What is Bill's monthly payment? What is the total interest cost of the loan?

15–3. Jim Smith took out a $60,000 mortgage on a ski chalet. The bank charged 3 points at closing. What did the points cost Jim in dollars?

15–4. Bill Jones bought a new split-level home for $190,000 with 20% down. He decided to use Victory Bank for his mortgage. They were offering $11\frac{3}{4}\%$ for 25-year mortgages. Could you provide Bill with an amortization schedule for the first month?

15–5. Janet Fence bought a home for $215,000 with a down payment of $50,000. The interest rate was $10\frac{1}{2}\%$ for 35 years. Calculate Janet's payment per $1,000 and her monthly mortgage payment.

15–6. Marvin Bass bought a home for $170,000 with a down payment of $20,000. His rate of interest is $11\frac{1}{2}\%$ for 25 years. Calculate Marvin's payment per $1,000 and his monthly mortgage payment.

15–7. Using Problem 15–6, calculate the total cost of interest for Marvin Bass.

15–8. Marsha Terban bought a home for $200,000 with a down payment of $40,000. Her rate of interest is 12% for 35 years. Calculate her (1) monthly payment, (2) first payment broken down into interest and principal, and (3) balance of mortgage at the end of the month.

15–9. Tom Burke bought a home in Virginia for $135,000. He puts down 20% and obtains a mortgage for 25 years at $12\frac{1}{2}$%. What is Tom's monthly payment and the total interest cost of the loan?

15–10. Susan Lake is concerned about the financing of a home. She saw a small cottage that sells for $60,000. If she puts 20% down, what will her monthly payment be at (1) 25 years, 10%; (2) 25 years, 11%; (3) 25 years, 12%; and (4) 25 years, 13%? What is the total cost of interest over the cost of the loan for each assumption?

CHAPTER 16

Self-Paced Worksheet

Cover the answers on the right and fill in each blank. After answering the question, look to the right for your answer.

Vocabulary Review

1. _____ represents the owner's investment in a sole proprietorship.
2. The _____ _____ is a financial report that lists assets, liabilities, and equity.
3. Things of value owned by a business are called _____.
4. The owner's equity of a corporation is called _____ _____.
5. _____ _____ is the amount of a corporation's earnings that the company retains in the business, not necessarily in cash form.
6. _____ _____ is a method of analyzing financial reports where each amount is compared to one total.
7. _____ _____ is a method of analyzing financial reports where each amount in this period is compared by amount and/or percent to same amount in the last period.
8. _____ _____ is equal to gross sales less sales discounts less sales returns and allowances.
9. Gross profit less operating expenses equals _____ _____.
10. _____ _____ involves analyzing each number as a percentage of a base year.
11. Current ratio is current assets divided by _____ _____.
12. _____ _____ is net sales divided by total assets.
13. _____ _____ is the relationship of one number to another.
14. Savings received by the buyer for paying for merchandise before a certain date are called _____ _____.

Theory Tips (and/or Cautions)

15. Capital does not mean _____.
16. Capital is not found in the _____ _____.
17. Current assets are consumed or converted into cash within _____ _____.
18. Companies use _____ and _____ assets in their business operation rather than for resale.
19. Land is an asset that doesn't _____.
20. Current liabilities are obligations that must be paid within _____ year.
21. Horizontal analysis needs comparative columns because we take the difference _____ periods of time.
22. The _____ _____ is a financial report that is prepared for a specific period of time.
23. The _____ _____ _____ _____ doesn't represent the selling price of goods sold by companies. It represents the cost of bringing the goods into the company.
24. Sales discounts are not the same as _____ discounts.
25. The base year in trend analysis is assumed to be _____ percent.
26. In the ACID test calculation, _____ and _____ expenses are subtracted.
27. The _____ _____ ratio analyzes if assets are being utilized efficiently.
28. Many companies compare their ratio analysis to _____ standard.

1.	capital
2.	balance sheet
3.	assets
4.	stockholders' equity
5.	retained earnings
6.	vertical analysis
7.	horizontal analysis
8.	net sales
9.	net income
10.	trend analysis
11.	current liabilities
12.	asset turnover
13.	ratio analysis
14.	purchase discounts
15.	cash
16.	stockholders' equity
17.	one year
18.	plant; equipment
19.	depreciate
20.	one
21.	between
22.	income statement
23.	cost of merchandise sold
24.	trade
25.	100
26.	inventory; prepaid
27.	asset turnover
28.	industry

Calculations/Applications

Do calculations on scrap paper as needed. Worked-out solutions are provided at end.

29. For Moore Corporation, calculate total stockholders' equity from the following: Cash, $8,000; land, $16,000; common stock, $18,000; accounts payable, $4,000; retained earnings, $6,000.

30. Complete vertical analysis (round to the nearest hundredth percent):

	2006	%	2007	%
Current assets:				
Cash	$ 15,000	A.	$ 18,000	D.
Accounts receivable	13,000	B.	5,000	E.
Merchandise inventory	42,000	C.	9,000	F.
Total current assets	$150,000		$120,000	

31. From the following information, calculate:
a. net sales; **b.** cost of merchandise (goods) sold; **c.** gross profit from sales; **d.** net income.

Gross sales, $42,000; sales returns and allowances, $4,000; beginning inventory, $8,000; net purchases, $9,000; ending inventory, $6,200; operating expenses, $8,400.

32. Prepare a trend analysis from the following, assuming a base year of 2003. Round to the nearest whole percent.

	2006	2005	2004	2003
Sales	$39,000	$65,000	$31,000	$40,000

33. **Given:** Total current assets, $20,000; accounts receivable, $8,000; total current liabilities, $12,000; inventory, $6,000; net sales, $40,000; total assets, $37,000; net income $8,400.
Calculate:
a. Current ratio (to nearest hundredth).
b. Acid test (to nearest hundredth).
c. Average day's collection.
d. Profit margin on sales.

29. $24,000

30. A. 10%
B. 8.67%
C. 28%
D. 15%
E. 4.17%
F. 7.5%

31. a. $38,000
b. $10,800
c. $27,200
d. $18,800

32. 2003: 100%
2004: 78%
2005: 163%
2006: 98%

33. a. 1.67
b. 1.17
c. 72 days
d. 21%

Worked-Out Solutions to Calculations/Applications Section

29. $18,000 + $6,000 = $24,000

30. A. $\dfrac{\$15,000}{\$150,000} = 10\%$ **D.** $\dfrac{\$18,000}{\$120,000} = 15\%$

B. $\dfrac{\$13,000}{\$150,000} = 8.67\%$ **E.** $\dfrac{\$5,000}{\$120,000} = 4.17\%$

C. $\dfrac{\$42,000}{\$150,000} = 28\%$ **F.** $\dfrac{\$9,000}{\$120,000} = 7.5\%$

31. a. $42,000 − $4,000 = $38,000
b. $8,000 + $9,000 − $6,200 = $10,800
c. $38,000 − $10,800 = $27,200
d. $27,200 − $8,400 = $18,800

32.

2006	2005	2004	2003
98%	163%	78%	100%
$\left(\dfrac{\$39,000}{\$40,000}\right)$	$\left(\dfrac{\$65,000}{\$40,000}\right)$	$\left(\dfrac{\$31,000}{\$40,000}\right)$	

33. a. $\dfrac{\$20,000}{\$12,000} = 1.67$ **b.** $\dfrac{\$20,000 - \$6,000}{\$12,000} = 1.17$

c. $\dfrac{\$8,000}{\dfrac{\$40,000}{360}} = 72 \; days$ **d.** $\dfrac{\$8,400}{\$40,000} = 21\%$

Word Problem Practice Quiz

Check with your instructor for complete worked-out solutions.

16–1. The total debt to total assets of the Jones Company was .91. The total of Jones' assets was $500,000. What is the amount of total debt to Jones Company?

16–2. Beaver Company has a current ratio of 1.88. The acid-test ratio is 1.61. The current liabilities of Beaver are $42,000. Could you calculate the dollar amount of merchandise inventory? Assume no prepaid expenses.

16–3. The asset turnover of River Company is 5.1. The total assets of River are $89,000. What are River's net sales?

16–4. Jangles Corporation has earned $79,000 after tax. The accountant calculated the return on equity as .14. What was Jangles Corporation's stockholders' equity?

16–5. In analyzing the income statement of Ryan Compay, cost of goods sold has decreased from 2005 to 2006 by 5.1%. The cost of goods sold was $15,900 in 2006. What was the cost of goods sold in 2005?

16–6. Don Williams received a memo requesting that he complete a trend analysis of the following using 2008 as the base year and rounding each percent to the nearest whole percent. Could you help Don with the request?*

	2005	2006	2007	2008
Sales	$440,000	$410,000	390,000	$400,000
Gross profit	180,000	200,000	240,000	250,000
Net income	$260,000	$210,000	$150,000	$150,000

*We assume no operating expenses.

16–7. Bill Barnes has requested that you calculate the asset turnover from the following (round answer to nearest tenth):

Gross sales	$55,000
Sales discount	$3,000
Sales returns and allowances	$2,000
Total assets	$34,000

16–8. Al Bean has requested you to calculate the cost of merchandise sold from the following: Sales, $52,000; beginning inventory, $2,800; purchases, $21,500; purchase discounts, $200; and ending inventory, $6,100.

16–9. The bookkeeper of Flynn Company has requested you to calculate the company's gross profit, based on the following: Sales, $28,100; sales returns and allowances $3,000; operating expenses, $5,100; beginning inventory, $700; net purchases, $9,000; and ending inventory, $1,200.

16–10. John's Pizza has an asset turnover of 2.8. The total assets were $80,000. What were the net sales of John's Pizza?

CHAPTER 17

Self-Paced Worksheet

Cover the answers on the right and fill in each blank. After answering the question, look to the right for your answer.

Vocabulary Review

1. Cost less accumulated depreciation equals _____ _____.

2. _____ is the process of allocating the cost of an asset (less residual value) over the asset's estimated life.

3. A table showing the amount of depreciation expense, accumulated depreciation, and book value for each period of time for a plant asset is called a _____ _____.

4. _____ value is the estimated value of a plant asset after depreciation is taken (or end of useful life).

5. _____ _____ is the amount of depreciation that has accumulated on plant and equipment assets.

6. The estimated number of years the plant asset is used is called its _____ _____.

7. _____ method of depreciation spreads an equal amount of depreciation each year over the life of the asset.

8. Sum-of-the-years'-digits and declining-balance are _____ methods of depreciation.

1.	book value
2.	depreciation
3.	depreciation schedule
4.	residual (salvage)
5.	accumulated depreciation
6.	useful life
7.	straight-line
8.	accelerated

Theory Tips (and/or Cautions)

9. _____ _____ cannot be less than residual value.

10. _____ can be indirect tax savings for the company.

11. Companies cannot depreciate _____.

12. Companies do not take the full month's depreciation for assets bought after the _____ of the month.

13. Units-of-production method is based on _____ rather than passage of time.

14. The numerator of the fraction in the sum-of-the-years'-digits calculation represents the _____ life.

15. The denominator of the fraction in the sum-of-the-years'-digits calculation remains the _____ for each calculation.

16. In the declining-balance method, you cannot depreciate below the _____ value.

17. To calculate depreciation expense in the declining-balance method, multiply the _____ _____ of equipment at _____ of year times depreciation rate.

18. In the declining-balance method, _____ _____ was not subtracted in the calculation.

19. MACRS is how a company records depreciation for _____ purposes.

9.	book value
10.	depreciation
11.	land
12.	15th
13.	usage
14.	remaining
15.	same
16.	residual
17.	book value; beginning
18.	residual value
19.	tax

Calculations/Applications

Do calculations on scrap paper as needed. Worked-out solutions are provided at end.

20. Given the following, calculate the yearly depreciation expense using the straight-line method.

    Truck, $30,000; residual value, $5,000; estimated useful life, 5 years.

21. On January 1, Lyon Co. bought a machine for $50,000 with an estimated life of 8 years. The residual value of the machine is $10,000. This machine is expected over its useful life to produce 60,000 units. This machine is expected to produce 9,000 units the first year and 16,000 in year 2. Calculate the depreciation expense for the machine in years 1 and 2.

22. Pete Smith bought a truck on January 1 for $60,000 with a residual value of $15,000. The truck has an estimated life of 5 years. Using the sum-of-the-years'-digits method, calculate the depreciation expense in years 1 and 2.

20.	$5,000 per year
21.	Year 1: $6,030 Year 2: $10,720
22.	Year 1: $15,000 Year 2: $12,000

23. If Pete in #22 bought the truck on April 5, what would the depreciation expense be in years 1 and 2?

24. If in #22 Pete used the declining-balance method at twice the straight-line rate, what would the depreciation expense be in years 1 and 2?

25. Using MACRS, what would be the first year's depreciation for a waste water sewer plant that cost $700,000?

23.	Year 1: $11,250
	Year 2: $12,750
24.	Year 1: $24,000
	Year 2: $14,400
25.	$35,000

Worked-Out Solutions to Calculations/Applications Section

20. $\dfrac{\$30,000 - \$5,000}{5 \text{ years}} = \dfrac{\$25,000}{5} = \$5,000$

21. $\dfrac{\$50,000 - \$10,000}{60,000} = \dfrac{\$40,000}{60,000} = \$.67$

   Year 1: 9,000 × $.67 = $6,030
   Year 2: 16,000 × $.67 = $10,720

22. $60,000
   −15,000
   ‾‾‾‾‾‾
   $45,000

   Year 1: $45,000 × $\dfrac{5}{15}$ = $15,000

   Year 2: $45,000 × $\dfrac{4}{15}$ = $12,000

23. Year 1: $15,000 × $\dfrac{9}{12}$ = $11,250

   Year 2: $15,000 × $\dfrac{3}{12}$ = $ 3,750

   $12,000 × $\dfrac{9}{12}$ = $\dfrac{9,000}{\$12,750}$

24. Year 1: $60,000 × .40 = $24,000
   Year 2: $60,000
       −24,000
       ‾‾‾‾‾‾
       $36,000 × .40 = $14,400

25. $700,000 × .05 = $35,000

Word Problem Practice Quiz

Check with your instructor for complete worked-out solutions.

17–1. Alvin Ross bought a truck for $7,000 with an estimated life of 4 years. The residual value of the truck is $1,000. Assume a straight-line method of depreciation. What will be the book value of the truck at the end of year 2? If the truck was bought on September 5, how much depreciation would be taken in year 1?

17–2. Jim Company bought a machine for $5,000 with an estimated life of 5 years. The residual value of the machine is $500. Calculate the (1) annual depreciation and (2) book value at the end of year 3. Assume straight-line depreciation.

17–3. Using Problem 17–2, calculate the first two years' depreciation assuming the units-of-production method. This machine is expected to produce 5,000 units. In year 1, it produced 2,400 units; in year 2, 2,600 units.

17–4. Assume Jim Company (Problem 17–2) used the sum-of-the-years'-digits method. How much more or less depreciation expense over the first two years would have been taken compared to straight-line depreciation?

17–5. Using Problem 17–2, calculate the first two years' depreciation assuming Jim Company used the declining-balance method at twice the straight-line rate.

17–6. Able Corporation bought a car for $6,750 with an estimated life of 7 years. The residual value of the car is $450. After 2 years, the car was sold for $5,200. What was the difference between the book value and the amount received from selling the car if Able used the straight-line method of depreciation?

17–7. If Able Corporation (Problem 17–6) used the sum-of-the-year's-digits method, what would have been the difference between the book value and the price at which the car was sold?

17–8. Jerry Jeves bought a new delivery truck for $6,800. The truck had an estimated life of 6 years and a residual value of $500. Prepare a depreciation schedule for the sum-of-the-years'-digits method.

17–9. Marika Katz, owner of Katz Ice Cream, is discussing with her accountant which method of depreciation would be best for her ice cream truck. The cost of the truck was $10,200, with an estimated life of 5 years. The residual value is $1,200. Marika wants you to prepare a depreciation schedule using the declining-balance method at twice the straight-line rate.

17–10. Morris Sullivan bought a machine for $6,900. Its estimated life is 5 years, with a $600 residual value. Using MACRS, calculate the depreciation expense per year for this machine over the first 3 years.

CHAPTER 18

Self-Paced Worksheet

Cover the answers on the right and fill in each blank. After answering the question look to the right for your answer.

Vocabulary Review

1. The last-in, first-out method (LIFO) assumes that the _____ inventory brought into the store will be the first sold.

2. The _____ _____ is an inventory method that estimates the cost of ending inventory by using a cost ratio.

3. _____ _____ is the total of all inventories divided by the number of times inventory was taken.

4. _____ _____ is a ratio that indicates how quickly inventory turns.

5. In a _____ inventory system, the inventory records are continually updated.

6. In a _____ inventory system, a physical count of inventory is taken at the end of a time period.

7. The _____ _____ method calculates the cost of ending inventory is taken by identifying each item remaining to the invoice price.

8. _____ expenses are not directly associated with a specific department or product.

9. The _____ _____ _____ uses the cost percentage to calculate the estimated cost of goods sold.

Theory Tips (and/or Cautions)

10. Companies that sell high cost items usually use the _____ _____ method of inventory valuation.

11. Companies with homogeneous products like fuels and grains may use the _____-_____ _____.

12. Cost of goods available for sale less cost of ending inventory equals _____ _____ _____ _____.

13. The cost flow assumption of FIFO or LIFO may or may not exist in the actual _____ flow of goods.

14. During inflation _____ produces a higher income than other inventory methods.

15. FIFO assumes that the first goods brought into the store are the _____ goods sold.

16. The retail method does not require that a company calculate an _____ cost for each item.

17. To use the _____ _____ method, the company must keep track of the average gross profit rate.

18. The inventory turnover at _____ is usually lower than the inventory turnover at _____.

19. A _____ inventory turnover might mean insufficient amounts of inventory resulting in stockouts.

20. The two common methods of calculating the distribution of overhead are by _____ _____ or _____ _____.

1.	last
2.	retail method
3.	average inventory
4.	inventory turnover
5.	perpetual
6.	periodic
7.	specific identification
8.	overhead
9.	gross profit method
10.	specific identification
11.	weighted-average method
12.	cost of goods sold
13.	physical
14.	FIFO
15.	first
16.	inventory
17.	gross profit
18.	retail; cost
19.	high
20.	floor space; sales volume

Calculations/Applications

Do your work on scrap paper as needed. Worked-out solutions are provided at end.

21. From the following calculate by the weighted-average method (a) the cost of ending inventory, and (b), the cost of goods sold. Ending inventory shows 18 units.

21. **a.** $66.24
    b. $139.76

		Number purchased for resale	Cost per unit	Total
January	1 inventory	12	$2	$24
March	1	9	$3	$27
April	1	20	$4	$80
November 1		15	$5	$75

22. Rework #21 using the FIFO assumption.

23. Rework #21 using the LIFO assumption.

24. Bill's Dress Shop's inventory at cost on January 1 was $32,500. Its retail value is $50,000. During the year, Bill purchased additional merchandise at a cost of $170,000 with a retail value of $366,000. The net sales at retail for the year was $345,000. Calculate Bill's inventory at cost by the retail method. Round the cost ratio to the nearest whole percent.

25. On January 1, Font Company had inventory costing $65,000 and during January had net purchases of $118,000. Over recent years, Font's gross profit has averaged 45% on sales. Given that the company has net sales of $190,000, calculate the estimated cost of ending inventory using the gross profit method.

22. a. $87
    b. $119
23. a. $42
    b. $164
24. $34,790

25. $78,500

Worked-Out Solutions to Calculations/Applications Section

21. $24 + $27 + $80 + $75 = $\dfrac{\$206}{56}$ = $3.68

    18 × $3.68 = $66.24 cost of ending inventory
    $206 − $66.24 = $139.76 cost of goods sold

22. 15 × $5 = $75
    3 × $4 = $\underline{\ \ 12}$
    $87 cost of ending inventory
    $206 − $87 = $119 cost of goods sold

23. 12 × $2 = $24
    6 × $3 = $\underline{\ \ 18}$
    $42 cost of ending inventory
    $206 − $42 = $164 cost of goods sold

24.

	Cost	Retail
Beginning inventory	$ 32,500	$ 50,000
Purchases	170,000	366,000
Cost of goods available for sale	$202,500	$416,000
Less net sales for the year		345,000
Ending inventory at retail		$ 71,000
Cost ratio $\dfrac{\$202,500}{\$416,000}$ = 49%		49%
Ending inventory at cost		$ 34,790

25.

Inventory, January 1		$ 65,000
Net purchases		118,000
Cost of goods available for sale		$183,000
Less: Estimated cost of goods sold:		
Net sales at retail	$190,000	
Cost percentage (100% − 45%)	.55	
Estimated cost of goods sold		$104,500
Estimated inventory, January 31		$ 78,500

Word Problem Practice Quiz

Check with your instructor for complete worked-out solutions.

18–1. Marvin Company has a beginning inventory of 7 sets of paints at a cost of $1.75 each. During the year, the store purchased 3 at $1.80, 7 at $2.50, 5 at $2.75, and 10 at $3.00. By the end of the year, 19 sets were sold. Calculate (1) the number of paint sets in stock and (2) the cost of ending inventory under LIFO.

18–2. Calculate the cost of ending inventory under FIFO for Problem 18–1. Round to nearest cent the average cost per unit before calculating the cost of ending inventory.

18–3. Calculate the cost of ending inventory by weighted average for Problem 18–1. Round to nearest cent the average cost per unit before calculating cost of ending inventory.

18–4. Jeffrey Company allocated overhead expenses to all departments on the basis of floor space (square feet) occupied by each department. The total overhead expenses for a recent year amounted to $90,000. Department A occupied 15,000 square feet; Department B, 5,000 square feet; Department C, 9,500 square feet. What is the amount of the overhead allocated to Department C? Round ratio to nearest whole percent.

18–5. In Problem 18–4, what amount of overhead is allocated to Department A? Round ratio to nearest percent.

18–6. Moose Company has a beginning inventory at a cost of $78,000 and an ending inventory costing $86,000. Sales were $410,000. Assume Moose's markup rate is 31%. Based on the selling price what is the inventory turnover at cost? Round to nearest hundredth.

18–7. May's Dress Shop's inventory at cost on January 1 was $38,500. Its retail value is $61,000. During the year, May purchased additional merchandise at a cost of $188,000 with a retail value of $402,000. The net sales at retail for the year was $352,000. Could you calculate May's inventory at cost by the retail method? Round cost ratio to nearest whole percent.

18–8. A sneaker shop has made the following wholesale purchases of new running shoes: 15 pairs at $26, 24 pairs at $27.50, and 8 pairs at $33.00. An inventory taken last week indicates that 17 pairs are still in stock. Calculate the cost of this inventory by FIFO.

18–9. The manager of Saikes Department Store is having difficulty calculating the inventory turnover at retail. The beginning retail inventory was $88,000 and the ending retail inventory was $96,000. The store's net sales were $715,000 and the cost of goods was $492,000. Assist the manager by computing the turnover to the nearest hundredth.

18–10. Over the past five years, the gross profit rate for Jerome Corp. wsa 42%. Using the gross profit method, estimate the cost of ending inventory given the following: Beginning inventory, $7,000; net purchases, $70,000; net sales at retail, $58,000.

CHAPTER 19

Self-Paced Worksheet

Cover the answers on the right and fill in each blank. After answering the question, look to the right for your answer.

Vocabulary Review

1. _____ _____ is the value of a property that an assessor sets that is used in calculating property taxes.

2. _____ _____ is a tax on specific luxury items or nonessentials.

3. A _____ is $\frac{1}{10}$ of a cent of $\frac{1}{1,000}$ of a dollar.

4. _____ _____ is a tax levied on consumers for certain sales of merchandise or services by states, counties, or various local governments.

5. _____ _____ is a tax that raises revenue for school districts, cities, counties, and the like.

6. Cars, home, furnishings, and jewelry are examples of _____ _____.

7. Land, buildings, and so on are examples of _____ _____.

1. assessed value

2. excise tax

3. mill

4. sales tax

5. property tax

6. personal property

7. real property

Theory Tips (and/or Cautions)

8. The list of items that is taxed for sales tax will _____ from state to state.

9. Trade discounts are subtracted from the _____ _____ before sales tax is computed.

10. The cost of shipping, handling, and so on are _____ subject to sales tax.

11. Sellers also take cash discounts on the _____ _____ before adding the sales tax.

12. _____ _____ is often calculated as a percentage of the selling price, although the tax can be stated as a fixed amount per item sold.

13. Real property and personal property are both subject to _____ _____.

14. In determining the tax rate, it should be _____ _____ to the indicated digit, even if it is less than 5.

15. To represent the number of mills as a tax rate per dollar, we divide the tax rate in decimal by _____.

16. In calculating property tax due, the total assessed value represents the _____.

17. In some states, a portion of assessed value is excluded from _____ _____ for senior citizens.

8. vary

9. original price

10. not

11. base price

12. excise tax

13. property tax

14. rounded up

15. .001

16. base

17. property tax

Calculations/Applications

Do calculations on scrap paper as needed. Worked-out solutions are provided at end.

18. John Sullivan, Jr., bought a new Apple computer for $1,900. The price included a 7% sales tax. What is (a) the sales tax and (b) the selling price before the tax?

19. In the community of Rose, the market value of a home is $150,000. The assessment rate is 40%. What is the assessed value?

20. Blooker County needs $910,000 from property tax to meet its budget. The total value of assessed property in Blooker is $141,000,000. What is the tax rate of Blooker? Round to the nearest ten thousandth. Express the rate in mills (to one tenth).

21. The home of Wally Waller is assessed at $75,000. The tax rate is 13.51 mills. What is the tax on Wally's home?

22. Lou's warehouse has a market value of $5,000,000. The property in Lou's area is assessed at 40% of the market value. The tax rate is $142.50 per $1,000 of assessed value. What is Lou's property tax?

18. a. $124.30
    b. $1,775.70

19. $60,000

20. 6.5 mills

21. $1,013.25

22. $285,000

Worked-Out Solutions to Calculations/Applications Section

18. $\dfrac{\$1,900}{1.07} = \$1,775.70$

$$\begin{array}{r} \$1,900.00 \\ -1,775.70 \\ \hline \$ \ \ 124.30 \end{array}$$

19. $\$150,000 \times .40 = \$60,000$

20. $\dfrac{\$910,000}{\$141,000,000} = .0064539 = .0065 \qquad \dfrac{.0065}{.001} = 6.5 \text{ mills}$

21. $13.51 \times .001 \times \$75,000 = \$1,013.25$

22. $\$5,000,000 \times .40 = \dfrac{\$2,000,000}{\$1,000} = $

$$\begin{array}{r} 2,000.00 \\ \times \ \$142.50 \\ \hline \$285,000.00 \end{array}$$

Word Problem Practice Quiz

Check with your instructor for complete worked-out solutions.

19–1. Tom Fall bought an $80 fishing rod that is subject to a 6% sales tax and a 12% excise tax. What is the total amount Tom paid for the rod?

19–2. Don Chater bought a new computer for $2,999. This included a 7% sales tax. What is the amount of sales tax and the selling price before the tax?

19–3. The Coffee Shop has a market value of $100,000. This property is assessed at 30% of the market value. The tax rate is $115.15 per $1,000 of assessed value. What is the property tax for the Coffee Shop?

19–4. Sheri Missan bought a ring for $8,000. She must still have to pay a 6% sales tax and an 8% excise tax. The jeweler is shipping the ring so Sheri must also pay a $30 shipping charge. What is the total purchase price of Sheri's ring?

19–5. Al's warehouse has a market value of $175,000. The property in Al's area is assessed at 45% of the market value. The tax rate is $119.20 per $1,000 of assessed value. What is Al's property tax?

19–6. In the community of Ross, the market value of a home is $210,000. The assessment rate is 28%. What is the assessed value?

19–7. Blunt County needs $690,000 from property tax to meet its budget. The total value of assessed property in Blunt is $105,000,000. What is the tax rate of Blunt? Round to nearest hundred thousandths. Express the rate in mills.

19–8. Bill Shass pays a property tax of $3,900. In his community, the tax rate is 47 mills. What is Bill's assessed value to the nearest dollar?

19–9. The home of Bill Burton is assessed at $90,000. The tax rate is 24.60 mills. What is the tax on Bill's home?

19–10. The building of Bill's Hardware is assessed at $118,000. The tax rate is $42.50 per $1,000 of assessed value. What is the tax due?

CHAPTER 20

Self-Paced Worksheet

Cover the answers on the right and fill in each blank. After answering the question, look to the right for your answer.

Vocabulary Review

1. The person(s) designated to receive the face value of the life insurance when the insured dies is called the _____.
2. _____ _____ represents the value of an insurance policy when terminated.
3. Inexpensive life insurance that builds up no cash value is called _____ _____.
4. _____ _____ is an insurance policy that is a combination of term insurance and cash value.
5. When a life insurance policy is terminated, _____ _____ include cash value, additional extended term, and/or additional paid-up.
6. _____ is a type of fire insurance in which the insurer and insured share the risk.
7. _____ represent the amount the insured pays before the insurance company pays.
8. Insurance required by law is called _____ _____.
9. _____ _____ is an optional auto insurance that pays for damages to the auto caused by factors other than from collison (fire, vandalism).
10. The _____ is the insurance company that issues the policy.

1.	beneficiary
2.	cash value
3.	term life
4.	20-year endowment
5.	nonforfeiture values
6.	coinsurance
7.	deductibles
8.	compulsory insurance
9.	comprehensive insurance
10.	insurer

Theory Tips (and/or Cautions)

11. Term insurance has no _____ _____.
12. An insurance company will never pay more than the _____ _____ of a policy.
13. Straight life insurance provides _____ protection.
14. Universal life insurance is basically a _____ _____ insurance plan with flexible premium schedules and benefits.
15. For straight life insurance, the longer the policy is in effect, the _____ the cash value because more premiums have been paid in.
16. In nonforfeiture options, the policy holder could get cash value, reduced paid-up insurance, or _____ _____ _____.
17. Life insurance is per $1,000, while fire insurance is per _____.
18. If the insurance company cancels your fire insurance they cannot use the _____-_____ _____. The result is more of a refund to the policyholder.
19. The bottom of the fraction in the calculation for coinsurance represents the _____ required to meet coinsurance. It is calculated by rate times replacement value.
20. _____ _____ covers injury to other people's autos, trees, buildings, etc.
21. 10/20 means the insurance company will pay damages to people injured or killed by your auto up to _____ for injury to one person per accident or a total of _____ for injuries to two or more people per accident.
22. If the policyholder lowers the deductible for collision comprehensive, an additional _____ results.
23. Premiums for collision, property damage, and comprehensive are not reduced by _____ _____.

11.	cash value
12.	face value
13.	permanent
14.	whole life
15.	higher
16.	extended term insurance
17.	$100
18.	short-rate table
19.	insurance
20.	property damage
21.	$10,000; $20,000
22.	premium
23.	no fault

Calculations/Applications

Do calculations on scrap paper as needed. Worked-out solutions are provided at end.

24. Alvin Hersey, age 44, purchased a $90,000, 5-year term life insurance policy. Calculate his annual premium. After 3 years, what is his cash value?
25. Gracie Lantz, age 44, purchased a $80,000 straight life policy. Calculate her annual premium.

24.	$405; no cash value
25.	$1,224

26. If after 15 years Gracie (problem #25) wants to surrender her policy, what options and what amounts are available to her?

27. Calculate the total annual premium of a building that has an area rating of 1 with a building classification A. The value of the building is $90,000, with contents valued at $40,000.

28. If the insured in problem #27 cancels at the end of month 8, what is the cost of the premium and the refund?

29. If in problem #28 the insurance company cancels at the end of month 8, what is the cost of the premium and the refund?

30. Ring insures a building for $160,000 with 80% coinsurance clause. The replacement value is $400,000. Assume a loss of $90,000 from fire. What will the insurance company pay?

31. Calculate the annual premium of Phil Smool who lives in territory 5 and is a classified driver 18, has a car with age 5 and symbol 2. His state has compulsory insurance and Phil wants to add the following options:

1. Bodily injury, 500/1000
2. Damage to someone else's property, 25M
3. Collision, 100 deductible
4. Comprehensive, 300 deductible
5. Towing

---

26. cash value: $11,840; paid-up, $29,680; extended: 20 yrs., 165 days

27. $392

28. premium: $290.08; refund: $101.92

29. premium: $261.33; refund: $130.67

30. $45,000

31. $865

Worked-Out Solutions to Calculations/Applications Section

24. $\dfrac{\$90,000}{\$1,000} = 90 \times \$4.50 = \$405$

25. $\dfrac{\$80,000}{\$1,000} = 80 \times \$15.30 = \$1,224$

26. Cash value: $80 \times \$148 = \$11,840$
Paid-up insurance: $80 \times \$371 = \$29,680$
Extended term: 20 year, 165 days

27. $\dfrac{\$90,000}{\$100}$ $\quad 900 \times \$.28 = \$252$

$\dfrac{\$40,000}{\$100}$ $\quad 400 \times \$.35 = \underline{\$140}$

$\qquad\qquad\qquad\qquad\qquad \$392$

28. Premium: $\$392 \times \$.74 = \$290.08$
Refund: $\quad\$392 \times \$.26 = \$101.92$

29. Premium: $\dfrac{8}{12} \times \$392 = \$261.33$

Refund: $\dfrac{4}{12} \times \$392 = \$130.67$

30. $\dfrac{\$160,000}{\$320,000} = \$.50 \times \$90,000 = \$45,000$

31. **Compulsory**

Bodily	$ 80
Property	$160

Options

Bodily	$251
Property	$166
Collision	$157 (124 + 33)
Comprehensive	$ 47
Towing	$ 4
Total	$865

Word Problem Practice Quiz

Check with your instructor for complete worked-out solutions.

20–1. Well-known actress Margie Rale, age 44, decided to take out a limited payment life policy. She chose this since she expects her income to decline in future years. Margie decided to take out a 20-year payment life policy with a coverage amount of $70,000. Could you advise Margie of what her annual premium will be? If she decides to stop paying premiums after 10 years, what would be her cash value?

20–2. Joyce Gail has two young children and wants to take out an additional $375,000 of 5-year term insurance. Joyce is 36 years old. What will her additional annual premium be? In 4 years, what cash value would have been built up?

20–3. Roger's office building has a $430,000 value, a rating of 1, and a building classification of A. The contents in the building are valued at $125,000. Could you help Roger calculate his total annual premium?

20–4. Carol Ellen's toy store is worth $50,000 and is insured for $30,000. Assume an 80% coinsurance clause and that a fire caused $20,000 damage. What is the liability of the insurance company?

20–5. Property of Al's Garage is worth $260,000. Al has a fire insurance policy of $200,000 that contains an 80% coinsurance clause. What will the insurance company pay on a fire that causes $108,000 damage?

20–6. Pete Williams had taken out a $69,000 fire insurance policy for his new restaurant at a rate of $.77 per $100. Seven months later, Pete canceled the policy and decided to move his store to a new location. What was the cost of the premium to Pete?

20–7. Earl Miller insured his pizza shop for $200,000 for fire insurance at an annual rate per $100 of $.75. At the end of 10 months, Earl canceled the policy since his pizza shop went out of business. What was the cost of Earl's premium and his refund?

20–8. Ron Tagney insured his real estate office with a fire insurance policy for $88,000 at a cost of $.48 per $100. Eight months later, his insurance company canceled his policy, because of a failure to correct a fire hazard. What did Ron have to pay for the 8 months of coverage? Round to nearest cent.

20–9. Jim Smith, who lives in Territory 5, carries 10/20/5 compulsory liability insurance along with optional collision that has a $500 deductible. Jim was at fault in an accident that caused $3,000 damage to the other auto, and $1,200 damage to his own. Also, the courts awarded $16,000 and $8,000, respectively, to the two passengers in the other car for personal injuries. How much will the insurance company pay, and what is Jim's share of the responsibility?

20–10. Marion Sloan bought a new jeep and insured it with only compulsory insurance 10/20/5. Driving up to her ski chalet one snowy evening, Marion hit a parked van and injured the couple inside. Marion's car had damage of $6,100, and the van she struck had damage of $7,500. After a lengthy court suit, the couple struck were awarded personal injury judgments of $17,000 and $8,100, respectively. What will the insurance company pay for this accident, and what is Marion's responsibility?

CHAPTER 21

Self-Paced Worksheet

Cover the answers on the right and fill in each blank. After answering the questions, look to the right for your answer.

Vocabulary Review

1. A _____ is one who owns stock in a company.
2. A _____ is a written promise by a company that borrows money, usually with fixed-interest payments until maturity (repayment time).
3. A _____ _____ is a cash distribution of the company's profit to owners of stock.
4. An _____ _____ is fewer than 100 shares.
5. The _____-_____ _____ is the closing price per share of stock divided by earnings per share.
6. The _____ _____ _____ is the annual earnings divided by the total number of shares outstanding.
7. _____ represents the distribution of company's profit in cash or stock to owners of stock.
8. _____ _____ _____ result when dividends accumulate when a company fails to pay dividends to cumulative preferred stockholders.
9. A _____ _____ results when a bond sells for less than the face value.
10. A _____ _____ results when a bond sells for more than the face value.
11. The _____ _____ _____ represents the dollar value of one share of a mutual fund.
12. A _____ _____ _____ is a mutual fund that has no sales charge.

Theory Tips (and/or Cautions)

13. _____ _____ _____ entitles its owners to a specific amount of dividends in a year. If not paid, these dividends in arrears accumulate.
14. _____ are allowed on the floor of the exchange.
15. _____ are traded in sixteenths of a dollar.
16. Bonds are traded in _____ of face amount and not in dollars like stock prices.
17. The _____-_____ _____ does not have one set number. It varies depending on earnings, expectations, economic conditions, etc.
18. A zero PE means the cmopany has _____ earnings.
19. When you buy or sell stock, a _____ charge results.
20. _____ _____ do not have the cumulative feature like preferred stockholders.
21. A bond may sell at a premium if the _____ rate is more attractive than other bonds.
22. The _____ _____ on a bond may be higher than the stated interest rate if one buys the bond at a discount.
23. No matter what _____ you pay for a bond, you will receive yearly interest (face value of bond times yearly interest).
24. For stocks or bonds, _____ close is not listed in today's quotation.
25. For a load fund, the _____ _____ is the NAV plus commission.
26. A front-end load would require the payment of a commission on _____ the shares, while a back-end load will pay the commission when the shares are redeemed.
27. The NAV is the _____ quote per share value.

1.	stockholder
2.	bond
3.	cash dividend
4.	odd lot
5.	price-earning ratio
6.	earnings per share
7.	dividend
8.	dividends in arrears
9.	bond discount
10.	bond premium
11.	net asset value
12.	no load fund
13.	cumulative preferred stock
14.	stockbrokers
15.	stocks
16.	percent
17.	price-earnings ratio
18.	no
19.	commission
20.	common stockholders
21.	interest
22.	current yield
23.	price
24.	yesterday's
25.	offer price
26.	purchasing
27.	closing

Calculations/Applications

Do calculations on scrap paper as needed. Worked-out solutions are provided at end.

28. Ellen Walters bought 400 shares of IBM stock at $56.25. Assume a commission of 5% of the purchase price. What is the total cost to Ellen?

29. Froll Company earns $6 per share; today the stock is trading at $66. The company pays an annual dividend of $.85. Calculate the (**a**) price-earning ratio and (**b**) yield on the stock (to the nearest tenth percent).

30. The stock of Lyon Co. is trading at $62.25. The price-earning ratio is 18 times the earnings. Calculate the earnings per share (to the nearest cent).

31. Alice Disney bought 5 bonds of AUT Company $8\frac{1}{2}06$ at 84 and 7 bonds of QUE Company at $9\frac{3}{4}02$ at 92. Assume the commission on the bonds is $4 per bond. What was the total cost of all purchases?

32. Janice Fall bought one bond for 128. The original bond was $8\frac{1}{4}08$. Calculate the current yield to the nearest tenth percent.

33. Cumulative preferred stockholders receive $.92 per share. There are 80,000 shares. For the last 4 years, no dividends have been paid. This year $280,000 is paid out in dividends. How much dividends to preferred is still in arrears?

34. Lee Winn buys 600 shares of a mutual fund with a NAV of $16.22. This fund has a load charge of 7%. What is the offer price and what did Lee pay for her investment?

28.	$23,625
29.	**a.** 11
	b. 1.3%
30.	$3.46
31.	$10,688
32.	6.4%
33.	$88,000 in arrears
34.	$17.36; $10,416

Worked-Out Solutions to Calculations/Applications Section

28. $400 \times \$56.25 = \$22,500 \times \$1.05 = \$23,625$

29. a. $\dfrac{\$66}{\$6} = 11$ **b.** $\dfrac{\$.85}{\$66} = 1.3\%$

30. $\dfrac{\$62.25}{18} = \$3.46$

31.
$5 \times \$840 = \$\ 4,200$
$7 \times \$920 = \underline{\$\ 6,440}$
$\$10,640 + \$48 = \$10,688$

32. $\$1,000 \times .0825 = \$82.50$

$\dfrac{\$82.50}{\$1,280} = 6.4\%$

33.
$80,000 \text{ shares} \times \$.92 = \$\ 73,600$
$\underline{\times\ 5}$
$\$368,000$
$\underline{280,000}$
$\$\ 88,000$

34.
$\$16.22 \times .07 = \$\ 1.14$
$\underline{+\ 16.22}$
$\$17.36$
600 shares $\times \$17.36 = \$10,416$

Word Problem Practice Quiz

Check with your instructor for complete worked-out solutions.

21–1. Norm Dorian bought 600 shares of CBS at $61.25 per share. Assume a commission of 3% of the purchase price. What is the total cost for Norm?

21–2. Assume in Problem 21–1 that Norm sells the stock for $71\frac{1}{8}$ with the same 3% commission rate. What is the bottom line for Norm?

21–3. Jim Corporation pays its cumulative preferred stockholders $2.50 per share. Jim has 40,000 shares of preferred and 80,0000 shares of common stock. In 2004, 2005, and 2006, due to slowdown in the economy, Jim paid no dividends. Now in 2006, the board of directors has decided to pay out $600,000 in dividends. How much of the $600,000 does each class of stock receive as dividends?

21–4. Roger Company earns $5.25 per share. Today the stock is trading at $61\frac{5}{8}$. The company pays an annual dividend of $1.95. Could you calculate the (1) price-earnings ratio (round to nearest whole number) and (2) the yield on the stock (to nearest tenth percent)?

21–5. The stock of VIC Corporation is trading at $70.75. The price-earnings ratio is 14 times earnings. Calculate the earnings per share for VIC Corporation to nearest cent.

21–6. Jerry Ryan bought the 6 bonds of Mort Company. $11\frac{1}{2}06$ at $91\frac{1}{2}$ and 4 bonds of Inst. System 12 S 09 for $88\frac{1}{4}$. If the commission on the bonds is $3.00 per bond, what was the total cost of all the purchases?

21-7. Sue Trenta bought 500 shares of a mutual fund with a NAV of $8.75. This fund has a load charge of 7%. What is (**a**) the offer price and (**b**) what did Sue pay for the investment?

21-8. Ron bought a bond for $88\frac{5}{8}$ of Bee Company. The original bond was $6\frac{3}{4}08$. Ron wanted to know the current yield to nearest tenth percent. Could you help Ron with the calculation?

21-9. Abby Sane decided to buy corporate bonds instead of stock. She desired to have the fixed-interest payments. She purchased 5 bonds of Meg Corporation $8\frac{7}{8}09$ at $89\frac{1}{2}$. As the stockbroker for Abby (assume you charge her a $5 commission per bond), provide her with the following: (1) the total cost of the purchase, (2) total annual interest to be received, and (3) current yield (to nearest tenth percent).

21-10. Mary Blake is considering whether to buy stocks or bonds. She has a good understanding of the pros and cons of both. The stock she is looking at is trading at $60.125, with an annual dividend of $3.65. Meanwhile, the bond is trading at $98\frac{1}{4}$ with an annual interest rate of 10%. Could you calculate for Mary her yield (tenth percent) for the stock and the bond, and make appropriate recommendations?

CHAPTER 22

Self-Paced Worksheet

Cover the answers on the right and fill in each blank. After answering the question, look to the right for your answer.

Vocabulary Review

1. A _____ _____ is a visual presentation using horizontal or vertical bars to make comparisons or to show relationships on items of similar makeup.

2. The _____ _____ is the current price divided by the base years price times 100.

3. A _____ _____ shows by table the number of times event(s) occurs.

4. The _____ is a statistical term that represents the central or midpoint of a series of numbers.

5. The _____ is a value that occurs most often in a series of numbers.

6. The _____ is an arithmetic average.

7. _____ _____ are graphical presentations that involve time elements.

8. The _____ _____ is intended to measure the spread of the data about the mean.

1. bar graph

2. price relative

3. frequency distribution

4. median

5. mode

6. mean

7. line graphs

8. standard deviation

Theory Tips (and/or Cautions)

9. When high or low numbers do not significantly affect a list of numbers, the _____ is a good indicator of where the center of the data occurs.

10. If high or low numbers have a significant effect on a list of numbers, the _____ may be better than the mean.

11. The _____ indicates where the center of data occurs without distorting a group of numbers with one or more extreme values.

12. The median in an odd number of values is the _____ value.

13. The median in an even number of values is the _____ of the two middle values.

14. Bar graphs can be _____ or _____.

15. _____ should be of equal size.

16. In a _____ _____ data is spread symmetrically about the mean.

9. mean

10. median

11. median

12. middle

13. average

14. vertical; horizontal

15. intervals

16. normal distribution

Calculations/Applications

Do calculations on scrap paper as needed. Worked-out solutions are provided at end.

17. Sales at Regan Realty totaled six homes for the week. They were as follows: $175,000; $180,000; $150,000; $190,000; $160,000; $90,000. Calculate the (a) mean and (b) median.

18. Computer Village counted the number of customers entering the store for a week. The results were: 1,095; 860; 1,095; 1,111; 865; 888; 1,000. What is the mode?

19. This semester, Dawn Pisai took four 3-credit courses at El Camino College. She received A's in Accounting and Business Math and B's in Logic and Psychology. What is her cumulative grade point average (assume A = 4; B = 3) to the nearest tenth?

17. a. $157,500
    b. $167,500

18. 1,095

19. 3.5

20. Jim's cleaners reported the following sales for the first 10 days of July:

$800	$900
$400	$600
$500	$100
$800	$200
$900	$300

Prepare a frequency distribution.

21. Irwin Publishing produced the following number of bound Business Math books during the first 5 weeks of last year:

Week	Bound books
1	5,000
2	2,000
3	3,000
4	4,000
5	1,000

Prepare a bar graph.

22. Kelly Industries reported record profits of 20%. It stated in the report that sales costs were 50% and expenses were 30%. Prepare a pie graph for Kelly.

23. Today, a new Ford Explorer costs $37,000. In 1991, the Explorer cost $18,700. What is the price relative to the nearest tenth percent?

24. Calculate the standard deviation of the following data (to nearest hundredth).

2 3 7 13 15

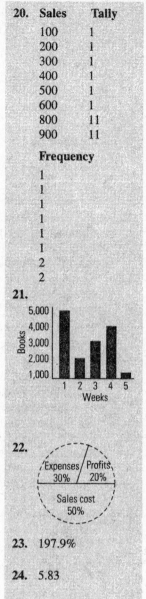

20.

Sales	Tally
100	1
200	1
300	1
400	1
500	1
600	1
800	11
900	11

Frequency

1
1
1
1
1
1
2
2

21.

22.

23. 197.9%

24. 5.83

Worked-Out Solutions to Calculations/Applications Section

17. a. $175,000
180,000
150,000
190,000
160,000
90,000
———
$945,000 ÷ 6 = $157,500

b. ($160,000 + $175,000) ÷ 2 = $167,500

19. 4 × 3 = 12
4 × 3 = 12
3 × 3 = 9 $\frac{42}{12}$ = 3.5
3 × 3 = 9
———
42

23. $\frac{37,000}{18,700}$ = 197.9%

24.

Data	Data − Mean	(Data − Mean)^2
2	2 − 8 = −6	36
3	3 − 8 = −5	25
7	7 − 8 = −1	1
13	13 − 8 = 5	25
15	15 − 8 = 7	49

$40 \div 5 = 8$ mean $\qquad\qquad$ $136 \div 4 = 34$

$\sqrt{34} = 5.83$

Word Problem Practice Quiz

Check with your instructor for complete worked-out solutions.

22–1. The batting averages of the North Shore Community College baseball team's starting 5 are: .333, .285, .395, .250. What is the team's mean batting average?

22–2. The following are the weights of 5 men who enrolled in a fitness class. What is the median weight of the men?

250 lbs.　　185 lbs.
290 lbs.　　165 lbs.
310 lbs.

22–3. Today, a new van costs $19,500. In 1980, the van cost $12,000. What is the price relative to the nearest tenth percent?

22–4. Marsha Horton received a quality point average of 3.2 for the semester from State Community College. She received 2 A's, 2 B's, and 1 C. All of her courses were 3 credits and A = 4, B = 3, C = 2, D = 1, and F = 0. Is her grade point average correct?

22–5. Marvin Shoes rang up the following sales for the day: $25, $10, $18, $25, $10, $30, $70, $70, $90, $18, and $25. What is the mode?

22–6. Foxes Gym holds an aerobics class twice a week. The weights of the participants are:

110 lbs.　　170 lbs.　　150 lbs.
190 lbs.　　180 lbs.　　130 lbs.
160 lbs.　　100 lbs.　　120 lbs.
160 lbs.　　130 lbs.　　110 lbs.
190 lbs.　　100 lbs.　　130 lbs.
130 lbs.　　120 lbs.　　140 lbs.

Construct a frequency distribution for Foxes Gym.

22–7. Using the frequency distribution in Problem 22–6, prepare a bar graph.

22–8. Morton's General Store divides its annual sales into categories as follows:

Food　　　32%
Medical　　49%
Services　　19%

If a circle graph was prepared, how many degrees would each section be?

22–9. Calculate the standard deviation of the following data to the nearest hundredth.

2　4　8　6　10

22–10. The following are dropout rates for Mr. Ryal's Accounting 1 class for the fall semester of each year:

2000	2001	2002	2003	2004	2005	2006
12%	15%	25%	16%	30%	28%	45%

Construct a line graph from this data.

Calculator Reference Guide

A QUICK REFERENCE GUIDE TO USING YOUR POCKET CALCULATOR*

[+] Plus key to add.   [×] Multiplication key.   [=] Completes calculation.
[−] Minus key to subtract.   [÷] Dividend key.

Topic	Manual example	Using your calculator	Display answer
Addition/subtraction	$15.842 + 3.2 - 24.642$	15.842 [+] 3.2 [−] 24.642 [=]	−5.6
Multiplication/division	$\dfrac{24 \times 26}{12}$	24 [×] 26 [÷] 12 [=]	52
Using a minus sign in multiplication	-14×46	14 [+/−] [×] 46 [=]	−644
Find the portion (using the percent key)	What is 35% of $800?	800 [×] 35 [%] *Note:* No equal sign is punched.	280
Find the rate	$280 is what percent of $800?	280 [÷] 800 [%]	35
Find the base	$280 is 35% of what number?	280 [÷] 35 [%]	800
Discounts	$500 less 5%	500 [−] 5 [%]	475
Adding on sales tax	$600 plus a 5% tax	600 [+] 5 [%]	630
A discount and a tax	$150 less 30% plus a 6% tax	150 [−] 30 [%] [+] 6 [%]	111.30
Simple interest	$1,200 \times 8\% \times \dfrac{60}{365}$	1200 [×] 8 [%] [×] 60 [÷] 365 [=]	15.780821
Using memory	$\dfrac{45}{3 \times 3}$	3 [×] 3 [=] [M +] 45 [÷] [MR] [=]	5
Memory used to solve principal using % key	$\dfrac{\$180}{11.5\% \times \dfrac{30}{360}}$	30 [×] 11.5 [%] [÷] 360 [=] [M+] 180 [÷] [MR][=]	18782.674
Same example without % key	$\dfrac{\$180}{.115 \times \dfrac{30}{360}}$	.115 [×] 30 [÷] 360 [=] [M+] 180 [÷] [MR][=]	18782.674

*Each calculator has variations—check your instruction booklet:

[+/−]   Changes sign of number from positive to negative or negative to positive.

[CE]   Clears last entry and NOT total.

[MC]   Clears memory.

[%]   Multiply by percent of the amount.

[M+]   Stored in memory (added).

[M−]   Subtracted from memory.

[MR]   Recalls what is stored in memory.

Reprinted by permission of Texas Instruments Incorporated.

TI BA II PLUS™ is a financial calculator that solves time-value-of-money calculations such as annuities, mortgages, and savings, and generates amortization schedules.

See the Texas Instruments Web site for features and Quick Guide at http://www.ti.com/calc/docs/baiip.htm

SAMPLE QUICK GUIDE REFERENCE

Payment and Compounding Settings (P/Y, C/Y)

The BA II Plus defaults to 12 payments per year (P/Y) and 12 compounding periods per year (C/Y). You can change one or both of the settings to any number. The examples below assume the BA II Plus is set to four decimal places.

To set both the P/Y and the C/Y to 1:

Press	Display	
2nd [P/Y] 1 ENTER	P/Y =	1.0000
↓	C/Y =	1.0000
2nd [QUIT]		0.0000

The above example shows annual compounding. You may want to set the P/Y to a different number than the C/Y. The following example shows how to set the BA II Plus for a monthly payment that is compounded quarterly.

To set the P/Y to 12 and the C/Y to 4:

Press	Display	
2nd [P/Y] 12 ENTER	P/Y =	12.0000
↓	C/Y =	12.0000
4 ENTER	C/Y =	4.0000
2nd [QUIT]		0.0000

The P/Y and C/Y settings continue indefinitely (even though the calculator is turned off and on), until you change them.

To calculate the future value of a dollar:

What is the future value of $1.00 invested for five years at an interest rate of 7% compounded annually? For this example, set P/Y and C/Y to 1.

Press	Display	
2nd [CLR TVM]		0.0000
1 +/− PV	PV =	−1.0000
5 N	N =	5.0000
7 I/Y	I/Y =	7.0000
CPT FV	FV =	1.4026

Clearing the Calculator

Clearing the calculator is different from resetting it. You can clear one or more values while retaining other data, whereas resetting the calculator clears all data and restores all settings to factory defaults.

To clear the calculator:

Press	To clear
→⃞	One character at a time (including decimal points)
CE/C⃞	An incorrect entry, an error condition, or error message
2nd⃞ [QUIT]	All pending operations in standard-calculator mode — or — Out of a prompted worksheet and return to standard-calculator mode (values previously entered remain in the prompted worksheet)
CE/C⃞ CE/C⃞	An unfinished calculation — or — A keyed, but not yet entered, variable value in a prompted worksheet — or — Out of a prompted worksheet and return to standard-calculator mode (values previously entered remain in the prompted worksheet)
CE/C⃞ 2nd⃞ [CLR TVM]	All values (N, I/Y, PV, PMT, FV) in the TVM (Time-Value-of-Money) worksheet
2nd⃞ [CLR Work]*	A prompted worksheet (other than TVM) Also returns you to the first variable in the worksheet
2nd⃞ [MEM] 2nd⃞ [CLR Work]*	All values stored in all 10 memories
O STO⃞ and the key for the number of the memory (0–9)	One memory

*You must be in the worksheet you want to clear before using 2nd⃞ [CLR Work]. Refer to the Notes section for each worksheet in the BA II Plus Guidebook to see how clearing affects specific worksheets.

© Copyright 1999 Texas Instruments Incorporated. All rights reserved.
Trademarks

Notes

Notes

Notes